WHAT THE HELL ...?
SO... ASAHINA-SAN ACTUALLY FIRED A LASER FROM HER EYE?
YES.
POU (POOF)
I WILL COMMENCE RESTORATION SHORTLY
I COULD ONLY GROAN.

6
THE MELANCHOLY of
HARUHI SUZUMIYA
ORIGINAL STORY
NAGARU TANIGAWA
MANGA
GAKU TSUGANO
CHARACTER DESIGN:
NOIZI ITO

CONTENTS

ONCE THIS MOVIE'S A SUCCESS, I'LL TAKE EVERYONE TO A HOT SPRING.
THINK OF IT AS A VACATION. A VACA-TION!
WHICH MEANS WE HAVE TO MAKE SOMETHING REALLY GOOD!
THEN WE'LL START FILMING AT THE SAME TIME TOMORROW.
IF YOU DON'T SHOW UP ON TIME, THERE WILL BE LYNCHING AND HEADS WILL ROLL!

WHICH MEANS THAT IT'S STORMING ALL AROUND US...

HONESTLY... IT'S ALWAYS QUIET IN THE EYE OF A HURRICANE.

I GUESS NAGATO SAVED MY LIFE AGAIN...

THIS TIME, WE HAD BEAMS SHOOTING OUT OF EYES.

YOU KNOW... KOIZUMI.

WE SHOULD BE FINE AS LONG AS HER EYE DOESN'T CHANGE COLORS...

ACCORDING TO THE SETTING, THE COLOR CONTACT IS THE SOURCE OF HER POWER.

I'LL LET ASAHINA-SAN KNOW LATER.

I FEEL LIKE THERE'S GOING TO BE A DISASTER IF WE KEEP FILMING.

I MEAN, I ALMOST DIED BACK THERE!

DO YOU INTEND TO LET HER KEEP SHOOTING THIS MOVIE?

HOWEVER, WE CANNOT SIMPLY CALL OFF THE MOVIE.

SHE IS ENJOYING THE CURRENT SITUATION...

ALMOST LIKE SHE'S PLAYING GOD...

THAT WHICH ISN'T POSSIBLE IN REALITY IS POSSIBLE IN FICTION.

SHE'S ABLE TO FREELY ENGAGE HER IMAGINATION AND CREATE HER OWN WORK.

GOD, IS IT?
I CAN'T EVEN BRING MYSELF TO LAUGH AT THIS POINT.
THIS TIME, THE ALTERATIONS TO REALITY ARE QUITE MODEST WHEN COMPARED WITH CELESTIALS.
IT WOULD SEEM BEST IF WE GO CASE BY CASE FOR THE TIME BEING...
FOR NOW, I SHALL GO PREPARE A SAFETY NET.
I'M SURE *SHE* WILL BE WILLING TO COOPERATE.
THEN I SHALL SEE YOU TOMORROW ...

LOOKS LIKE THIS MESS WON'T BE ENDING ANYTIME SOON.
WILL I BE ABLE TO SURVIVE UNTIL IT DOES...?
PURURURU (RRRING)
HELLO? IT'S ME.
BRING THOSE GUYS WITH YOU TOMORROW.

THE NEXT DAY
HEY, KYON! THIS ISN'T HOW YOU SAID IT WOULD BE.
WHERE'S THE LOVELY ASAHINA?
SFX: DON (BAM)
I CAME HERE FOR THE EYE CANDY!
THERE, THERE, THERE.
HOW WOULD I KNOW?
MORNING, KYON-KUN!
GOOD GRIEF... WE'VE GOT ANOTHER NOISE-MAKER ON OUR HANDS.
HARUHI HAD CALLED FOR THREE EXTRAS IN TOTAL.

OH, MIKURU ISN'T HERE YET—

WHAT ARE YOU TALKING ABOUT!?

SO, HEYAS! WHAT'RE WE DOING?

WHY'S YUKI-CHAN DRESSED LIKE THAT!?

I WON'T ACCEPT THAT EXCUSE!

WHAT? YOUR STOMACH HURTS?

YOU'RE THE STAR!

I'LL HAVE TO GO RUN HER DOWN!

YOU GUYS WAIT HERE.

WAKYA

わきゃ

WAKYA

わきゃ

WAKYA

わきゃ

WAKYA (YAP)

WAKYA

わきゃ

ARE WE HOLDING A SHOUTING CONTEST THIS MORNING ...?

GOU
(VROOM)

I CAN UNDERSTAND HOW ASAHINA-SAN FEELS.

YES... WE WON'T HAVE TO WORRY ABOUT THAT, AT LEAST.

IT WON'T BE FUNNY IF MORE LASERS SHOOT OUT.

I'M NOT SURE WHAT SHE SPECIFICALLY DID...

I REQUESTED THAT SHE NULLIFY ANY RISK.

I ASKED NAGATO-SAN FOR HER ASSIS-TANCE.

HUH?

SHE SPEAKS VERY LITTLE.

UNLIKE THE OTHER T.F.E.I. TERMINALS.

YOU'RE NOT SURE?

THAT'S NOT VERY RESPONSIBLE.

IN ANY CASE, SHE MAY BE MORE THAN A MERE INTERFACE... PERHAPS.

OH... EXCUSE ME.

T.F...?

BATAN (SLAM)

IT APPEARS THAT OUR DIRECTOR HAS RETURNED.

BURURURURU (BRRROOM)

OH?

I BELIEVE THAT SHE MAY PLAY A DIFFERENT ROLE...

SORRY ABOUT BEING LATE...
WOW, AMAZ-ING! SEXY!
WHAT'S WITH THE COSTUME? ARE YOU ACTING IN THIS!?
GU (CLENCH)
YOU'RE NOT GOING TO GET AWAY WITH PRETENDING TO BE SICK.
SORRY...
MIKURU-CHAN, THIS WILL BE YOUR TIME TO SHINE.
LET'S HEAD OVER, THEN!

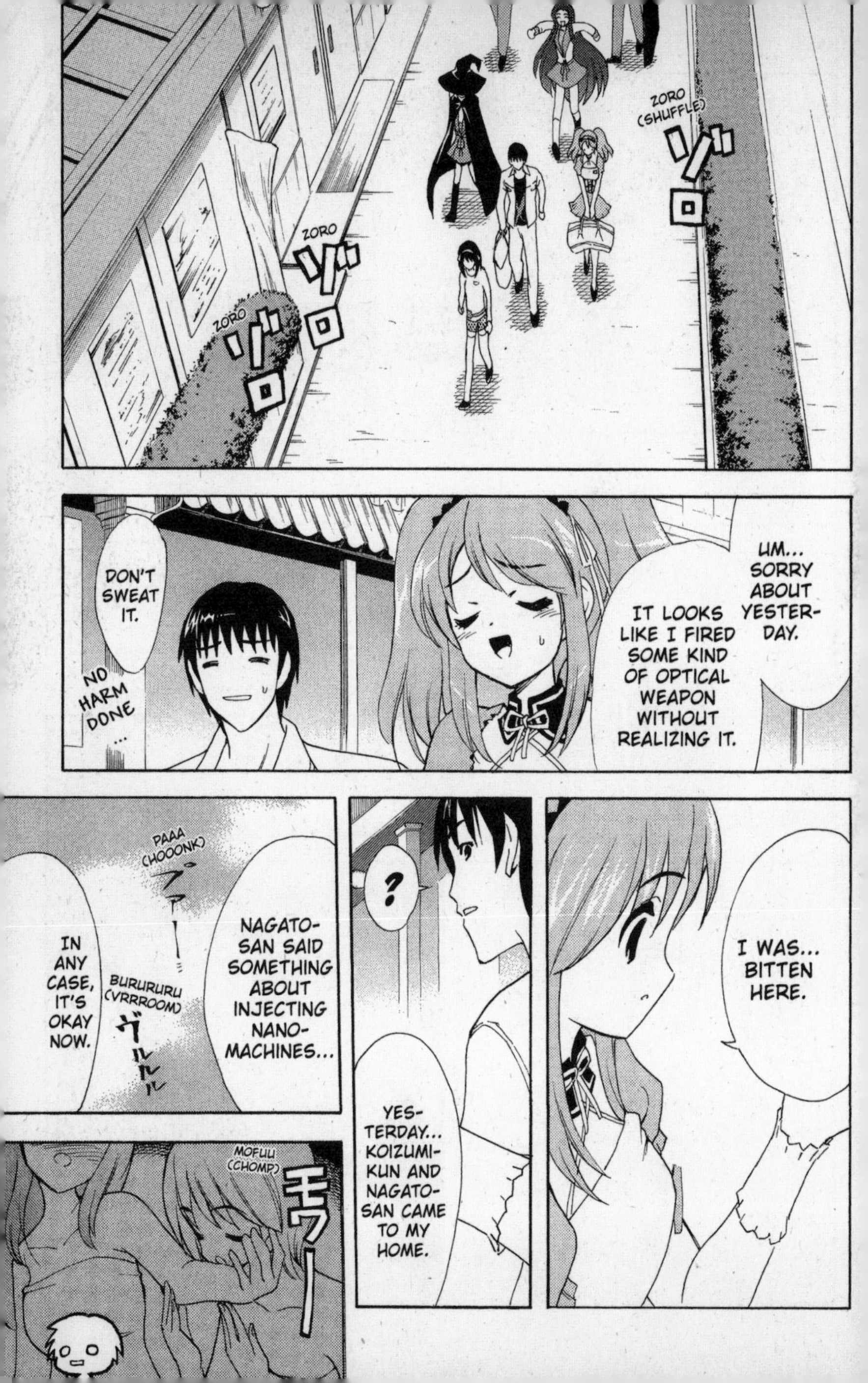
ZORO (SHUFFLE)
ZORO
ZORO
UM... SORRY ABOUT YESTER-DAY.
IT LOOKS LIKE I FIRED SOME KIND OF OPTICAL WEAPON WITHOUT REALIZING IT.
DON'T SWEAT IT.
NO HARM DONE...
I WAS... BITTEN HERE.
?
YES-TERDAY... KOIZUMI-KUN AND NAGATO-SAN CAME TO MY HOME.
NAGATO-SAN SAID SOMETHING ABOUT INJECTING NANO-MACHINES...
PAAA (HOOONK)
IN ANY CASE, IT'S OKAY NOW.
BURURURU (VRRROOM)
MOFUU (CHOMP)

...DOESN'T MAKE MUCH SENSE, BUT FOR SOME REASON, I WISH I HAD BEEN THERE TO SEE IT...
OKAY! IT'S FINALLY TIME FOR THE SCENE WHERE MIKURU'S IN A BIG PINCH.
WE'LL CALL IT: "MIKURU VS. SLAVE PUPPETS"!
MIKURU FIGHTS FOR JUSTICE, SO SHE CAN'T HARM NORMAL PEOPLE...
YUKI IS TAKING ADVANTAGE OF THAT WEAKNESS BY TURNING ORDINARY PEOPLE INTO HER SLAVES.
YOU LOT ARE THE SLAVE PUPPETS!
SOUNDS SO FUN!

GRAB HER BY HER ARMS AND LEGS AND TOSS HER IN!

!?

START BY THROWING MIKURU-CHAN INTO THE POND.

COULD WE AT LEAST USE A WARM-WATER POOL?

ANY FOOL CAN SEE IT'S FILTHY.

HEY... INTO THIS POND?

U... UM, I'LL ...

EASY FOR YOU TO SAY...

PON (PAT)

SHUT UP!

SACRIFICES MUST BE MADE FOR THE SAKE OF REALISM.

THAT'S WHAT I WOULD EXPECT FROM A HAND-PICKED BRIGADE MEMBER!

HEY! MIKURU-CHAN, THAT'S GREAT!

I-I-I-I'LL DO IT!

YOU'VE REALLY GROWN. I'M SO THRILLED.

ASAHINA-SAN...

...SHE MUST BE HEART-BROKEN.

THREE ...TWO...

START!

...SHOULD WE REALLY BE LETTING HER RUN LOOSE?

STILL...

ONE WRONG MOVE AND HARUHI WILL MAKE WEIRD STUFF HAPPEN...

OKAY, GET READY!

PRE-PARE YOUR-SELF!
SORRY, MIKURU.
HIEE (SHRIEK)
I REALLY DON'T WANT TO DO THIS...
...BUT WE'RE BEING MIND-CONTROLLED AND STUFF ...!
W-WAIT, ACTUALLY, IS THIS REALLY NECES-SARY?
NOOOOOO!
AGHHH...
READY, AND...
SORRY, MIKURU-CHAN.
IT'S TO MAKE THE SCENE BETTER... YES.

DOBBOON (KERSPLASH)
...FOR THE SAKE OF ART.
ASAHINA-SAN...A REALLY GOOD JOB OF ACTING LIKE YOU'RE DROWNING.
EEP!
BASHA (SPLASH)
BASHA
AHBU!
GAH HAH!
BASHA
HUH? SOMEONE ELSE FELL IN.
NOBODY CARES.
...BUT, DOESN'T ASAHINA-SAN LOOK LIKE SHE'S SERIOUSLY IN TROUBLE?
HELP HER ALREADY!
HOGYAAA!
BASHA
BASHA
I GET IT.
KOIZUMI-KUN, IT'S YOUR TURN!

CALM DOWN.

TRY NOT TO DRAG ME IN AS WELL... YES.

BASHA

BASHA

BASHA

QUICK, GRAB ON.

BASHA

KIRA

ARE YOU ALL RIGHT?

KIRAA
(SPARKLE)

WAH... I'M SAVED.

I SWALLOWED WA—GAH BAH!

LET ME FILM SOME MORE.

HEY, HARUHI!

PER-FECT!

CUT!

SCREEN: PLAY, TIME REMAINING:
YEP.
AH-CHOO!
再生
01:43
JIIIII (STAAARE)
THE SCENE OF THEIR MEETING WAS ADEQUATE.
YOU CAN FEEL HOW AWKWARD THEY ARE AROUND EACH OTHER.
REALLY? KOIZUMI LOOKS THE SAME AS ALWAYS.
HEYA THERE ...
MY HOUSE IS CLOSE BY.
MIKURU LOOKS LIKE SHE'S ABOUT TO CATCH A COLD, SO CAN I GET HER A CHANGE OF CLOTHES?

WHAT A SMOOTH TURN OF EVENTS!

WE CAN FILM A SCENE WHERE ITSUKI AND MIKURU GET FRIENDLY THERE.

HUH?

TSURU-CHA...

THAT'S IT, TSURU-CHAN!

HEBUSHI (SNEEZE)

WHAT SHOULD WE DO?

UH... UMM...

THE FILM GODS MUST BE SMILING ON ME!

SFX: NIKO (SMILE)

DOOON GLUOOM

EH...

...HARUHI CONSIDERS THE TWO OF THEM WORTHLESS.

IT SEEMS THAT...

OKAY, LET'S GO.

TSURU-CHAN, HURRY UP AND SHOW US THE WAY!

THANKS FOR YOUR HARD WORK!

LUCKY FOR THEM.
...SO LATER, HAVE ...
... READY, OKAY?
AH-HA-HA-HA!
THAT'S A RIOT!
WHAT IS THIS... THEY'RE GETTING ALONG REALLY WELL.
WHAT ARE THEY PLOTTING ...?
OKAY! WE'RE HERE!
THIS IS MY HOUSE!
THAT WAS CLOSE!
...OR WAIT, BEFORE THAT...

FI FI FI
CHI
(TWEE)
CHI
CHI

A RATHER TRADITIONAL OLD HOME.

REFINEMENT IN ITS BEARING... YOU CAN FEEL ITS AGE.

IT'S HUGE!

YOU CAN WAIT OVER THERE IN MY ROOM!

I'LL GET MIKURU INTO A BATH.

......

HERE. COME ON IN.

WHAT IS GOING ON HERE...
KAPOOON (BADUUUM)
...A SURPRISING TURN OF EVENTS.
WE HAVE TO MAKE USE OF THIS CHANCE.
DEFI-NITELY A SURPRISE...
THIS IS CRAZY STUFF.
MAKES MY HOME LOOK LIKE A DOG-HOUSE...
WE'LL SAY THIS IS ITSUKI'S ROOM.
AND THEN...
I'D ALWAYS THOUGHT THAT SHE WAS A NORMAL PERSON WITH A LOUD VOICE.
THIS MIGHT BE A STRETCH...
...BUT IS SHE ALSO "SOMEBODY SPECIAL"?

WHOA...

HAVE YOU RECOV-ERED?

AH.

UM... SORRY TO KEEP EVERYONE WAITING.

NOW, NOW... HOW ABOUT SOME JUICE?

S-SOME-WHAT.

YES... I'VE BEEN WORKING ALL DAY.

YOU MUST HAVE BEEN THIRSTY.

I NO LONGER CARE ABOUT ANY OF THE STUPID QUESTIONS I HAD.

IS THAT ONE OF TSURUYA-SAN'S T-SHIRTS?

GOKU (GULP)

GOKU

KYU (WHEW)

TH-THAT'S HOT...

OKAY, IT'S TIME TO FILM THE NEXT PART.

YOU'RE TALKING OUT LOUD.

NOT THAT I REALLY CARE. NOT THAT I HAVE TIME TO WORRY ABOUT THAT.

WELL, SHE'S PROBABLY A NORMAL PERSON.

WHAT...? ALREADY?

ガシャ
GASHA (RUSTLE)
す
SU (SWSH)
すぅ
SUUU (ZZZ)

YEP... THAT'S GOOD.

LOVE THE MOOD.

JIII (STARE)

THIS IS KIND OF GETTING ON MY NERVES...

WE'RE GETTING TO THE MEAT OF THE STORY.

A WEAKENED MIKURU... AND ITSUKI TAKING CARE OF HER.

ARE YOU AWAKE?

UH... MMM...

YEAH...

ASAHINA-SAN... LOOKING AWFULLY SEXY.

AH ...!
ころん
KORON (FALL)
THANK YOU VERY MUSH.
EXACTLY WHAT I WANTED.
NOW, YOU TWO! GET CLOSE TOGETHER!
HEY... HOLD ON.
IS THIS ACTING?
CLOSER, CLOSER ...
AS CLOSE AS YOU CAN GET!

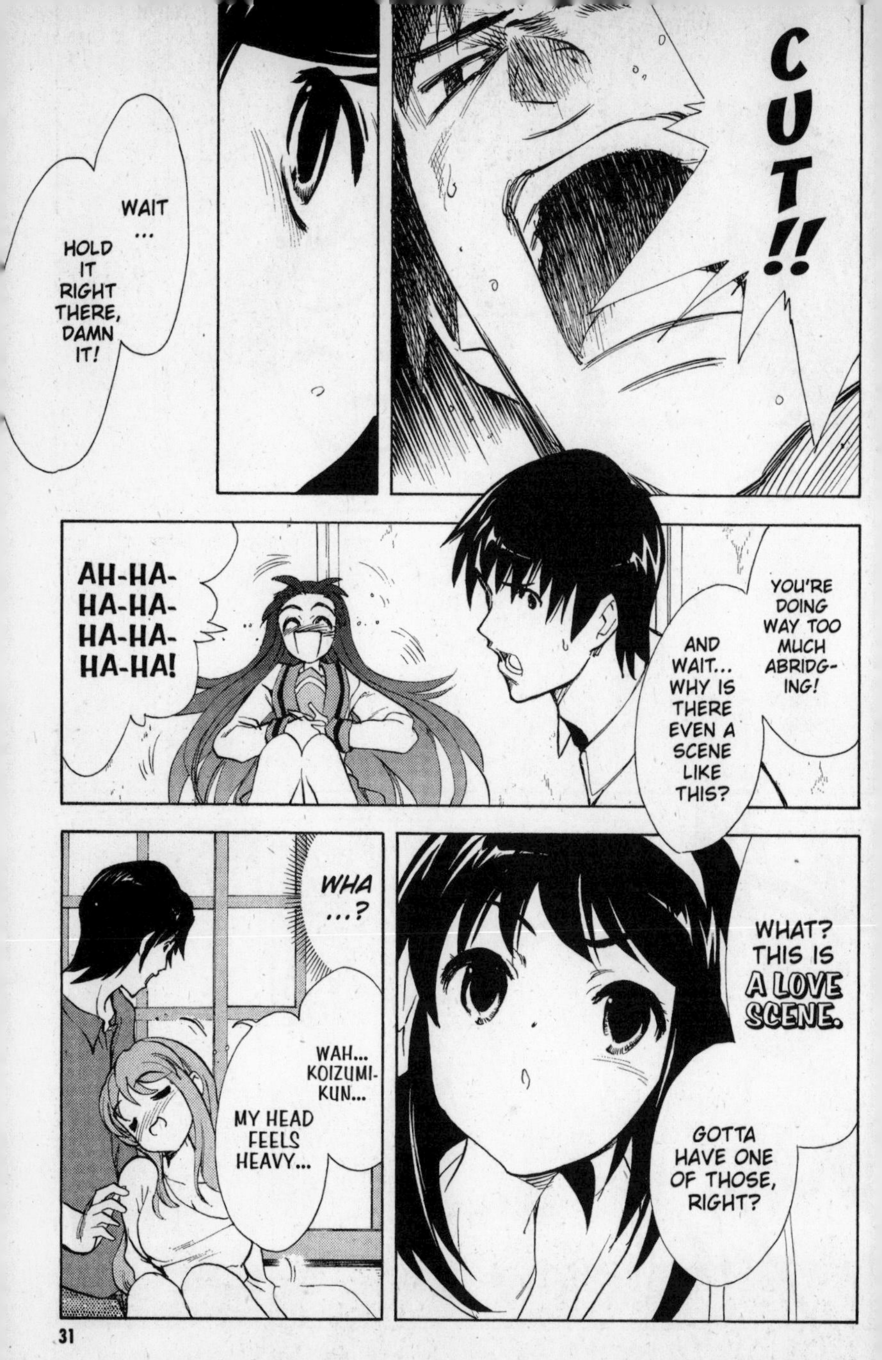
CUT!!
WAIT ... HOLD IT RIGHT THERE, DAMN IT!
YOU'RE DOING WAY TOO MUCH ABRIDG-ING!
AND WAIT... WHY IS THERE EVEN A SCENE LIKE THIS?
AH-HA-HA-HA-HA-HA-HA-HA!
WHAT? THIS IS A LOVE SCENE.
GOTTA HAVE ONE OF THOSE, RIGHT?
WHA ...?
WAH... KOIZUMI-KUN... MY HEAD FEELS HEAVY...

SORRY!
I MIXED TEQUILA INTO MIKURU'S JUICE.
I WAS TOLD THAT SOME ALCOHOL MIGHT HELP HER ACTING.
I WAS ABSOLUTELY RIGHT!
MIKURU-CHAN LOOKS REALLY SEXY RIGHT NOW.
......
SO THAT'S WHAT IT WAS.
OKAY, NOW'S OUR CHANCE TO GET A KISS SCENE IN.
OF COURSE, I MEAN ON THE LIPS!
GASHA (CRASH)

HELL NO!
WHY ARE YOU SUCH A KILLJOY?
I'M MERELY FOLLOWING CONVEN-TION.
WHAT CONVENTION!? THIS ISN'T AMUSING AT ALL.
GETTING HER DRUNK... HOW DOES THAT EVEN WORK?
ASAHINA-SAN ISN'T YOUR TOY!
I'VE DECIDED THAT SHE IS!
MIKURU-CHAN IS MY TOY!

BISHI (SMACK)
......
...IMPULSE OVERCAME REASON.
I JUST SNAPPED.
WHAT ...

WHAT IS YOUR PROBLEM !?
YOU SHOULD JUST DO AS I SAY!
I'M THE BRIGADE CHIEF AND DIRECTOR AND...
ANYWAY, I WON'T ALLOW YOU TO GO AGAINST ME!!
DAMN IT...!
BA (SHOVE)
WAH, PLEASE STOP!!

YOU MUSTN'T FIGHT...
EVERY-BODY HAS TO GET ALONG TOGETHER ...
...OR ELSE ...
HMM... THIS WAS CLASSIFIED ...

...GOOD GRIEF.
I EXPECTED YOU TO BE A MORE COMPOSED PERSON...
KO (CLACK)
THAT'S WHAT I THOUGHT TOO.
KO
WE ALREADY HAVE ENOUGH IRREGU-LARITIES IN THE REAL WORLD TO DEAL WITH.
KO
I WOULD RATHER YOU REFRAIN FROM ANY ACTIONS THAT WOULD LEAD TO THE CREATION OF CLOSED SPACE.

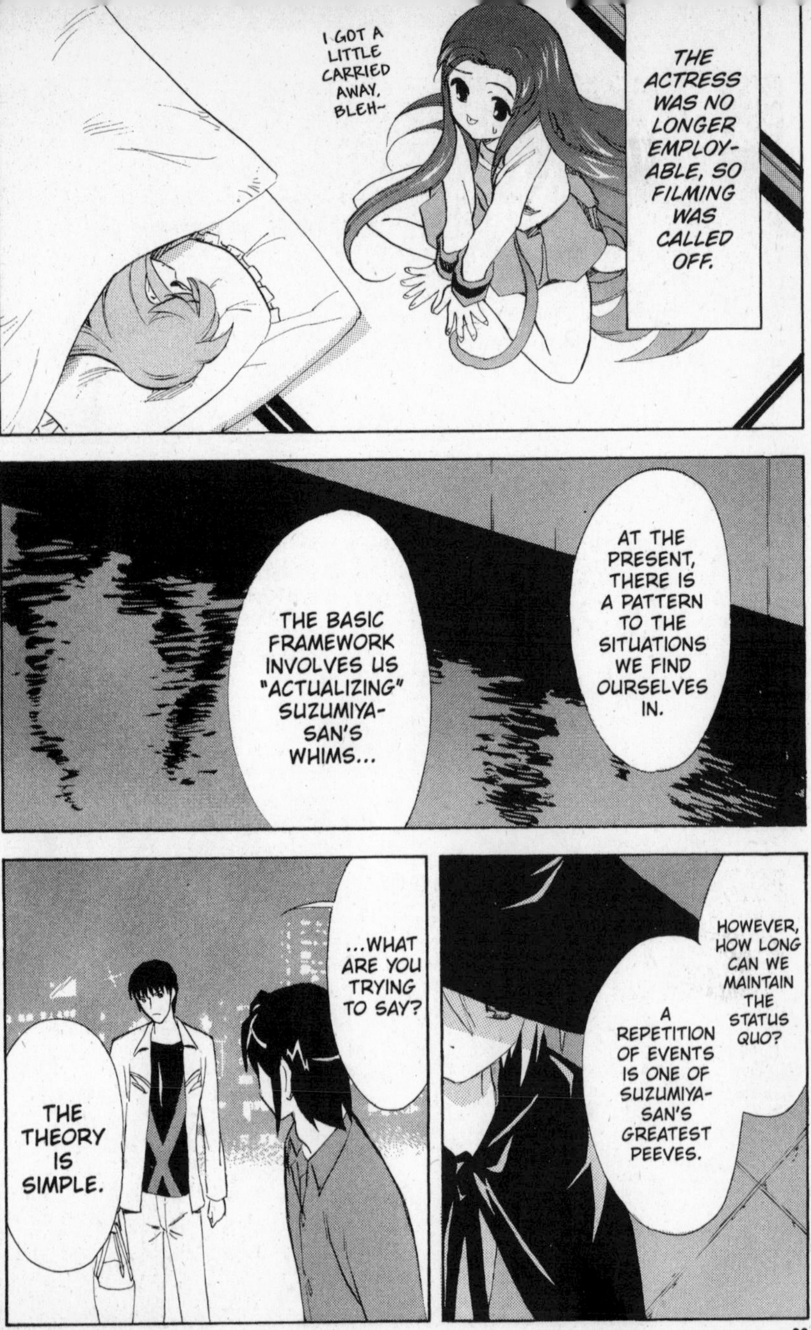

THE ACTRESS WAS NO LONGER EMPLOYABLE, SO FILMING WAS CALLED OFF.
I GOT A LITTLE CARRIED AWAY, BLEH~
AT THE PRESENT, THERE IS A PATTERN TO THE SITUATIONS WE FIND OURSELVES IN.
THE BASIC FRAMEWORK INVOLVES US "ACTUALIZING" SUZUMIYA-SAN'S WHIMS...
HOWEVER, HOW LONG CAN WE MAINTAIN THE STATUS QUO?
A REPETITION OF EVENTS IS ONE OF SUZUMIYA-SAN'S GREATEST PEEVES.
...WHAT ARE YOU TRYING TO SAY?
THE THEORY IS SIMPLE.

WE SERVE AS HARUHI SUZUMIYA'S *TRANQUIL-IZER.*

...

WE MUST PREVENT THE INFRINGE-MENT OF "DELUSION" INTO "REALITY."

WE MUST DO OUR BEST TO KEEP HER IN A PLACID STATE...

WHENEVER SHE HAS AN IDEA, THERE IS A RIPPLE EFFECT IN THE "REAL WORLD."

NOT NECES-SARILY.

THEN I WOULDN'T HAVE TO WORRY ABOUT THIS STUPID STUFF.

I WISH I WERE A CAT.

OH?

THERE'S NO REASON FOR YOU TO EVEN ATTEMPT TO CONSIDER OUR WORRIES.
FROM OUR PERSPECTIVE, HUMAN CONCERNS ARE MUCH MORE INSIGNIFICANT.
HOWEVER, THERE IS NO POINT IN LESSER LIFE FORMS ARGUING THAT FACT.
IT WOULD BE CARELESS TO IGNORE INDIVIDUAL THOUGHT BY STEREOTYPING AN ENTIRE SPECIES.
....
GUESS I SPOKE TOO SOON... HUH?

THE SIGH OF HARUHI SUZUMIYA III : END

THIS IS WHAT HAPPENS AFTER THEY'VE LIVED SO MANY YEARS?

IS THIS A CAT-DEMON-TYPE CREATURE?

I DO NOT KNOW THE ANSWER.

I HAVE NO INTEREST IN DIFFERENTIATING BETWEEN THE PRESENT AND PAST.

I SHALL CONTACT ASAHINA-SAN AGAIN.

...WHAT A QUANDARY.

IT'S TALKING IN A DEEP VOICE.

THE SIGH OF HARUHI SUZUMIYA IV

HOWEVER, PARROTS AND PARAKEETS ARE CAPABLE OF DOING THE SAME.

I AM CERTAINLY EMITTING SOUNDS THAT RESEMBLE HUMAN SPEECH.

......

YOU ARE ABSOLUTELY RIGHT.

NOBODY WOULD KNOW WHETHER OR NOT ACCURATE COMMUNICATION OCCURRED, CORRECT?

HOW CAN YOU BE SURE THAT WE ARE HOLDING A CONVERSATION?

THIS SITUATION...

...DOESN'T LOOK VERY ENCOURAGING.

SORRY, BUT COULD YOU STOP TALKING AND HOLD ON FOR A MINUTE?

WHY ARE WE HAVING SUCH AN ACADEMIC CONVERSATION WITH A CAT...?

WE APPEAR TO HAVE UNDER-ESTIMATED SUZUMIYA-SAN.
I FEAR THAT THE SETTING WITHIN THE MOVIE IS BECOMING THE "CONVENTIONAL REALITY" OF THIS WORLD.
BETWEEN BEAMS SHOOTING FROM EYES AND CATS TALKING.
WE JUST HAVE TO MAKE SURE THAT HARUHI DOESN'T FIND OUT, RIGHT?
ORIGI-NALLY, YES.
HOWEVER, A LARGE QUANTITY OF "UNREALITY" HAS BEGUN TO SHROUD THIS SPACE.
WHAT DO YOU MEAN?

DIDN'T YOU NOTICE ANYTHING AS YOU WATCHED THE PREPARATIONS FOR THE CULTURAL FESTIVAL?
THERE WERE MORE AND MORE PEOPLE IN FANTASY GARB EVERY DAY.
WELL, YEAH.
THE CULTURAL FESTIVAL IS COMING UP...
INDEED...
FOR US, SUZUMIYA'S POWER COULD BE CONSIDERED SIMILAR TO A "ZASHIKI-WARASHI."
WE SHOULD BE ACQUAINTED WITH ALL OF THE HUMANS PRESENT.
HOWEVER, A HEAD COUNT REVEALS THAT A FEW EXTRA PEOPLE HAVE BEEN MIXED IN...
OUR CURRENT SITUATION IS FILLED WITH SUCH DISCREPANCIES.

A TALKING CAT APPEARING AT THIS PARTICULAR MOMENT...

I PRESUME THAT IT CANNOT BE ENTIRELY UNRELATED TO THE STRESS FROM YOUR FIGHT.

WE MUST QUICKLY DEVISE A RATIONAL ENDING FOR THIS MOVIE.

END-ING?

SORRY ABOUT THAT...

AT THIS RATE, WE HAVE A SNOWBALL EFFECT.

THE CONTENTS OF THE FILM ARE INFRINGING ON THE "REAL WORLD."

ELEMEN-TARY.

UTTERLY LOGICAL AND SIMPLE.

WHAT KIND OF ENDING?

HUH!?
BA (SLAM)
......
OH... IT WAS JUST A DREAM.
STILL... BEAMS SHOOTING FROM EYES AND CATS TALKING ...
I MUST BE TIRED.

IT WAS ALL JUST A DREAM!?

ISN'T THAT SIMPLE?

YES.

GI (CREAK)

UNFOR-TUNATELY...

...WE NO LONGER HAVE TIME FOR SUCH INDUL-GENCES.

SHE'S NOT GOING TO ALLOW SUCH A BLATANT CLICHÉ.

SHE'S GOING ON AND ON ABOUT WINNING THAT AWARD.

...YOU THINK HARUHI WILL ACCEPT THAT?

...IS THE BEST WAY TO SETTLE THE MATTER.

DEEMING THAT EVERYTHING IN THE MOVIE WAS A DREAM, LIE, OR MISTAKE...

THIS RESOLUTION WAS DETERMINED BY OUR NEEDS.

HOW SHE FEELS IS NOT RELEVANT.

...BUT THERE'S A CONTRADICTION IN THAT IDEA.

WELL, IT MIGHT BE BETTER FOR ME TOO...

FOR YOU, MAYBE.

....

WEREN'T YOU THE ONE WHO SAID THAT...
...HARUHI UNDERSTOOD HOW THE SUCCESS OF THE MOVIE RESTED ON ITS SUBSTANCE?
SHE WON'T ALLOW AN ENDING THAT SHE DOESN'T ACCEPT.
THAT WOULD ONLY GIVE HARUHI MORE STRESS.
......
...THAT'S A PROBLEM.
I WAS ALREADY AWARE OF THE ISSUE WHEN I MADE THAT SUGGES-TION...
AFTER SEEING HER TANTRUM TODAY...
...I DOUBT SHE'LL ACCEPT YOUR PROPOSAL.

THEN OUR ONLY CHOICE IS TO CALL THE FILM OFF.
CONVINCE HER TO ACCEPT A HIGH-HANDED ENDING... OR CALL IT OFF.
THOUGH THE RISK REMAINS.

....

SICK OF THIS... I'M SICK OF ALL OF THIS.

KO (KNOCK)

... HMM?

DAMN IT...

WE WERE FILMING THIS MOVIE TO PUT HER IN A BETTER MOOD.

CALL OFF THE MOVIE BECAUSE HARUHI'S IN A BAD MOOD?

DAN (SLAM)

GI (SQUEAK)

THE LAST OF THREE COMMERCIALS TO BE BROADCAST THROUGHOUT THE SCHOOL.

...OH, YEAH.

THERE'S THIS TAPE.

THIS ONE'S SUPPOSED TO BE SHOWN TOMORROW?

TAPE: SUPER ULTRA TOP-SECRET AND VALUABLE FOOTAGE NUMBER 3

WHAT TO DO?

SHOULD I SET IT ASIDE AS UNNECESSARY CLUTTER...?

MIGHT BE BETTER NOT TO SHOW THIS...

...SO WE DON'T CREATE ANY NEEDLESS EXPECTATIONS.

THE NEXT DAY
KOOON (DOOONG)
CHI (TWEE)
CHI
CHI
GARARA (RATTLE)
... HARU-HI.
...THERE'S NO REASON FOR ME TO APOLOGIZE.
....

YOU LEARN YOUR LESSON ...
...FROM YESTER-DAY?
GATAN (CLATTER)
......
I HAVE NO INTENTION OF WORSHIPPING HER THE WAY KOIZUMI DOES.
...SAY SOME-THING.
WE WON'T BE ABLE TO CONTINUE FILMING IF YOU'RE LIKE THAT.
OR DO YOU WANT TO CALL IT OFF?
......
MUNZU (YANK)
PASA (FLUTTER)

WAH!

TSUKA

TSUKA

TSUKA
(STRIDE)

SFX: DON (SHOVE)

BAN
(BANG)

WHEN DO WE START FILMING TODAY...

HUH?

WHAT'S WRONG WITH SUZUMIYA-SAN TODAY?

......

I SEE.

MAYBE SOMETHING HAPPENED TO PISS HER OFF.

BEATS ME.

SO MUCH FOR FILMING ...
HMM ...
IS THIS HOW IT'S GOING TO END?
BUT... SHE LOOKED MORE UPSET ...
...THAN ANGRY TO ME.
...OH YEAH.
WHY DID SHE HAVE A PONYTAIL TODAY?

ONE MORE HOUR UNTIL IT'S TIME TO BROAD-CAST THE COMMER-CIAL, HUH...
I GUESS THIS VIDEO'S GETTING SHELVED.
KYON-KUN!
MIKURU HAS SOME-THING FOR YOU!
?
UM ...
PLEASE TAKE THIS!

COUPON: MAID YAKISOBA CAFÉ, DOUBLE DEVA, ¥200 OFF, "COME ON TOPKNOT"

IT'S A DISCOUNT VOUCHER FOR OUR CLASS'S YAKISOBA CAFÉ.
メイド焼きそ
仁王
200円割引
来てちょんまげ
P-PLEASE INVITE YOUR FRIENDS TO COME ALONG.
THAT'S ALL!
SEE YA!
HUH? OH, I SEE...
PEKO (BOW)
ぺこー
?
MOJI (FIDGET)
もじもじ
MOJI
UM ...
KYON-KUN, DO YOU HAVE A MOMENT?
YES?
EH HEH HEH HEH!

ACTUALLY... ABOUT WHAT HAPPENED YESTERDAY.

UM!

I HOPE YOU DON'T TAKE THIS THE WRONG WAY, BUT...

WELL...IT CONCERNS SUZUMIYA-SAN'S POWER.

NO...

YOU MEAN THE FIGHT?

WELL...

UM...I WAS WONDERING IF IT MIGHT HAVE A LASTING EFFECT...

...MY "INTERPRE-TATION" IS DIFFERENT FROM KOIZUMI-KUN'S.

I'M SORRY IF I SOUND LIKE I'M BAD-MOUTHING HIM...

YOU REALLY SHOULDN'T... TRUST WHAT KOIZUMI-KUN SAYS.

IT'S TRUE THAT SUZUMIYA-SAN HAS THE POWER TO ALTER THE PRESENT.
HOWEVER... I DON'T BELIEVE SHE'S CHANGING THE STRUCTURE OF THE WORLD.
THE WORLD WAS LIKE THIS TO BEGIN WITH.
IT WASN'T CREATED BY SUZUMIYA-SAN.
I BELIEVE THAT... NAGATO-SAN HAS A SIMILAR VIEW.
I'M SORRY... I'M BAD AT EXPLAINING THINGS.
UH...
SO BASICALLY, YOUR PERSPECTIVE IS AT ODDS WITH KOIZUMI'S?

KOIZUMI-KUN HAS HIS OWN CIRCUM-STANCES TO DEAL WITH.
THE SAME GOES FOR US...AND PROBABLY FOR NAGATO-SAN AS WELL.
THAT IS WHY ...
......
I UNDER-STAND.

W C
U-UM... KYON-KUN.
THANK YOU FOR LISTENING TO ME.
BUT I DON'T HOLD ANYTHING AGAINST KOIZUMI-KUN.
PLEASE UNDERSTAND THAT.
I SEE... HUH.
JAA (FLUSH)

MIKURU ASAHINA'S TENET COULD BE EXPLAINED AS FOLLOWS.
HARUHI SUZUMIYA IS NOT THE CREATOR.
THE WORLD ALWAYS EXISTED IN ITS CURRENT FORM.
ESPERS, ALIEN LIFE FORMS... ALL ORIGINALLY EXISTED.
THEY WERE NOT BORN AS A RESULT OF HARUHI SUZUMIYA'S WISHES.
MAN... HOW LONG WAS SHE LISTENING TO US?
I CAN'T EVEN GO TO THE BATHROOM IN PEACE...

HARUHI SUZUMIYA'S POWER WOULD BE THE ABILITY TO DISCOVER SUCH ENTITIES.
AND ELEMENTS EXIST TO PREVENT THE RECOGNITION OF THAT POWER.
THAT WOULD BE US.
HMM...
THIS IS GETTING COMPLICATED.
SO ASAHINA-SAN...FOR A REASON DIFFERENT FROM KOIZUMI'S...
...ALSO DOESN'T WANT HARUHI TO NOTICE...
YES.

HARUHI SUZUMIYA IS CONSIDERED A VARIABLE TO SPACE-TIME...
$y=x$
IN ORDER TO MAINTAIN THE STABILITY OF THE FUTURE, IT IS NECESSARY TO INPUT THE CORRECT VALUES.
MIKURU ASAHINA'S ROLE IS TO REGULATE THOSE VALUES.
$y=h_1x$
$y=h_3x$
$y=h_2x$
......
...I GUESS... I KIND OF UNDER-STAND.
BUT KOIZUMI SAID THAT HIS ESP SHOWED UP THREE YEARS AGO?
THAT WOULD MEAN HIS POWER DIDN'T ORIGI-NALLY EXIST.
HOW DO YOU EXPLAIN THAT CONTRA-DICTION?

SIMI-LARLY...

...THE BREAK-THROUGH SOLUTION OFFERED YESTERDAY IS NOT UNCONDITIONAL.

THERE IS NO GUARANTEE THAT ITSUKI KOIZUMI IS TELLING THE TRUTH.

......

NAGATO.

DOES IT NEED TO BE ELIMINATED?

KOIZUMI WANTS TO CHANGE THE ENDING OF THE MOVIE.

WHAT DO YOU THINK?

......
ANY TRUTH I MAY TELL YOU WILL NOT GRANT...
...SOLID PROOF...
FOR THERE IS NO GUARANTEE THAT I AM TELLING THE TRUTH.

...NOT FOR YOU, AT LEAST.
...I SEE.
NO-BODY KNOWS HOW THE MOVIE WILL GO...
AAAAAA (SPLASH)

ジャアア
アアア
JAAAAAA (SPLASH)
KOIZUMI'S PLAN ISN'T GUARANTEED TO WORK.
THE SAME GOES FOR ASAHINA'S VIEW...
AND IF I CAN'T RELY ON NAGATO ...
I'VE NEVER SEEN THAT LOOK ON HER FACE BEFORE.
AH... KYON-KUN.
IS THAT THE VIDEO FOR THE COMMERCIAL?

WHAT SHOULD WE DO?
IF THE MOVIE'S GOING TO BE CANCELED... WE SHOULDN'T SHOW THE COMMERCIAL.
I'VE BEEN DOING SOME THINKING.
I'M SORRY TO SAY THAT THIS THING'S GETTING *SHELVED*.
HUH ...?
SO THAT MEANS...
I CAN'T ACCEPT IT.
NOT AFTER THAT ARBITRARY DIRECTING.
YES.

WE'RE MAKING A NEW TAPE TO REPLACE THIS ONE.
BEFORE IT'S TIME TO BROAD-CAST!
SORRY, BUT ASAHINA-SAN... COULD YOU GIVE ME A HAND?
?
HUH?

I CAN'T ACCEPT IT.

...I WON'T LET THE FILM BE CANCELED NOW...!

The Sigh of Haruhi Suzumiya IV : END

WE'RE MAKING A NEW TAPE TO REPLACE THIS ONE.
BEFORE IT'S TIME TO BROAD-CAST!
超㊙ 極㊙ お宝映像 その3
WH- WHAT DO YOU MEAN?
OH!
DO YOU MEAN A VIDEO WHICH LETS EVERYBODY KNOW THAT THE MOVIE'S BEEN CANCELED!?
NO...
I WON'T LET YOU CALL THIS OFF, HARUHI...
YOU NEED TO FINISH THIS MOVIE.

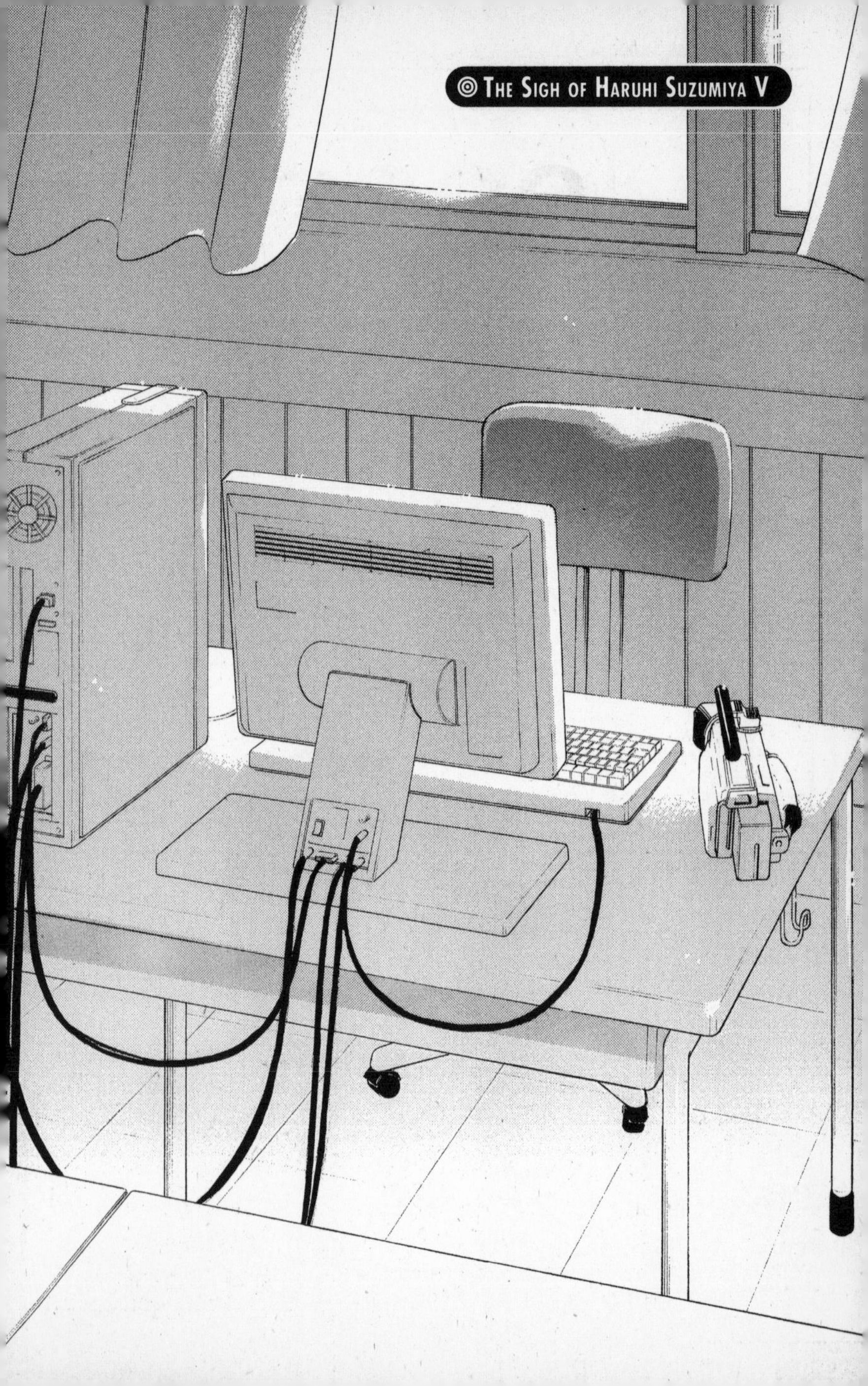

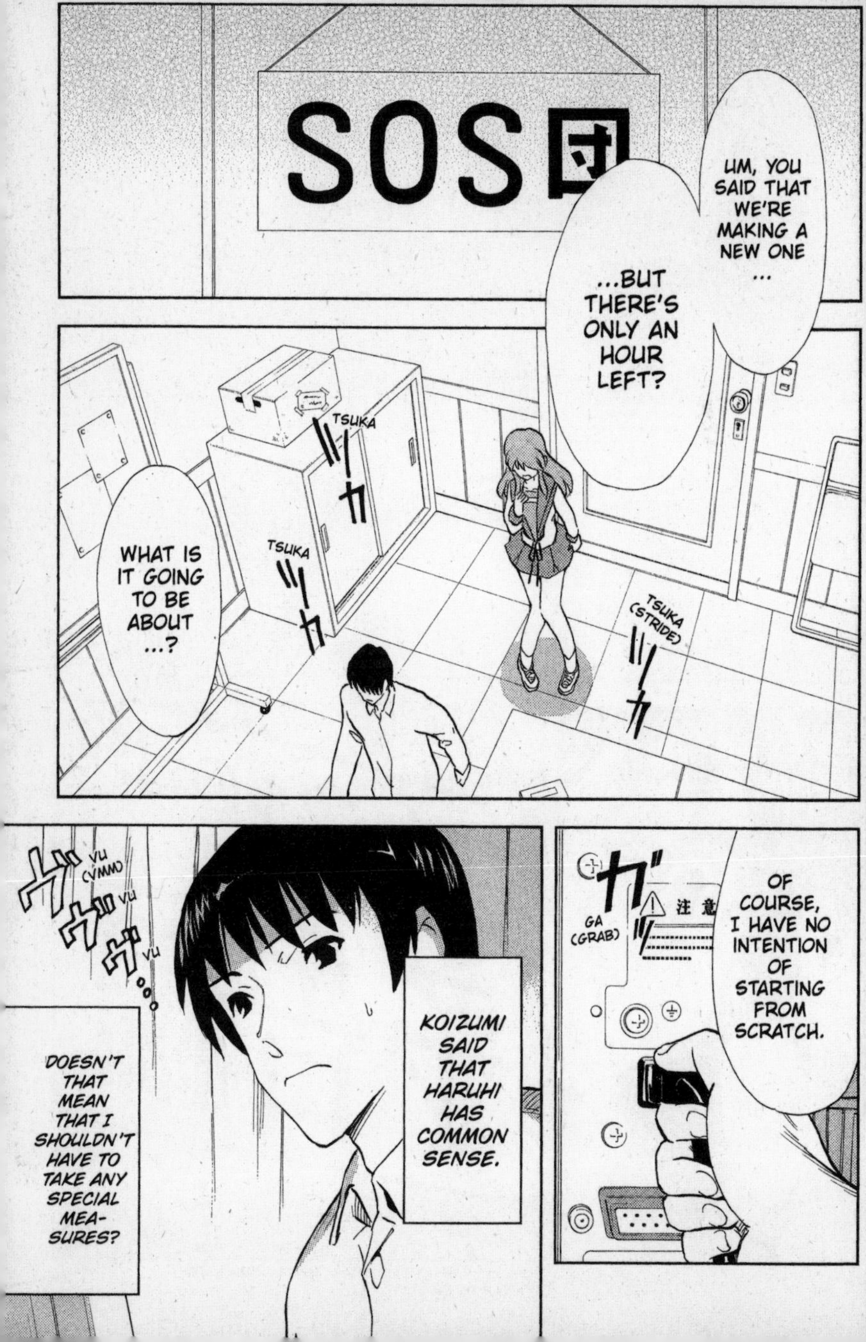

SOS団

UM, YOU SAID THAT WE'RE MAKING A NEW ONE ...

...BUT THERE'S ONLY AN HOUR LEFT?

WHAT IS IT GOING TO BE ABOUT ...?

TSUKA

TSUKA

TSUKA (STRIDE)

VU (VMMO)

VU

VU

VU

DOESN'T THAT MEAN THAT I SHOULDN'T HAVE TO TAKE ANY SPECIAL MEASURES?

KOIZUMI SAID THAT HARUHI HAS COMMON SENSE.

GA (GRAB)

注意

OF COURSE, I HAVE NO INTENTION OF STARTING FROM SCRATCH.

ピンポーン
PIN (DING)
POOON (DOONG)
This is the noon broadcast.
Today's cultural festival promotion features the SOS Brigade with their third appearance!
朝比奈ミクルの冒険
EPISODE 00
予告編
PONY
BAN (BAM)
HUH!?

SCREEN: "THE ADVENTURES OF MIKURU ASAHINA EPISODE 00 PREVIEW"

I am an alien mage.

WE SOMEHOW MADE IT IN TIME!

BROAD-CASTING ROOM

SINCE THIS WAS JUST A COMPILATION OF THE FOOTAGE WE SHOT.

ZUBIBAAN (SHAAPOW)

Who are you!?

SIGN: BROADCASTING ROOM

TSUKA

TSUKA (STRIDE)

TSUKA

WELL, THIS IS A BET OF SORTS.

BUT IF EVERYTHING GOES AS EXPECTED...

BUT IS IT OKAY TO DO THIS?

WE DIDN'T TELL SUZUMIYA-SAN THAT WE WERE GOING TO SHOW A PREVIEW...

...AND WE DON'T KNOW IF THE MOVIE WILL EVEN BE FINISHED.

YOU GUYS!

ZUBAAN (SLAM)

DIDN'T WE SHOOT THE THIRD COMMERCIAL ALREADY!? THIS WASN'T PART OF THE PLAN!

WHAT ARE YOU BROADCASTING WITHOUT MY PERMISSION!?

WHAT? DIDN'T I TELL YOU?

WAH... THIS WAS PROBABLY A BAD IDEA.

I FIGURED THIS WOULD BE MORE EFFECTIVE THAN THOSE SHOPPING DISTRICT COMMERCIALS.

HUH?

EH ...?

Mikuru Beam!

BY THE WAY, HARUHI ...

...WERE YOU HAVING FUN AS WE FILMED THE MOVIE?

KYON-KUN...

HOW CAN YOU ACT LIKE YOU NEVER FOUGHT ...?

THIS STUFF ISN'T SO BAD...

THIS WHOLE MOVIE-MAKING BUSI-NESS...

I WAS PRETTY SKEPTICAL WHEN YOU CAME UP WITH THE IDEA...

...BUT WE MANAGED TO COME THIS FAR.

Re take

O-OF COURSE.
ANYTHING WE MAKE HAS TO BE ENTERTAINING.
SO WHY ARE YOU SO MAD?
...
BECAUSE THAT WASN'T ENOUGH!
HAND ME THE MIC!
BA (WHAP)
ITTON: SPEAKER ON.
PI (BEEP)
放送ON
!?

GA (THNK) GA GA
Ahem!
PII (SCREE)
Attention all students!
GA GA
Loaded with top-top-top-secret footage of Mikuru Asahina!
GA GA GA
The biggest film of the year, presented by the SOS Brigade.
PII
Viewers will come swarming!!
GA GA
朝比奈ミクルの冒険
EPISODE 00
予告編
SCREEN: "THE ADVENTURES OF MIKURU ASAHINA EPISODE 00 PREVIEW"
YOU'LL DEFINITELY REGRET IT IF YOU MISS IT!
IT'LL BE TOO LATE AFTERWARD...!!
......

A PREVIEW ONLY WORKS WHEN THERE'S A TAGLINE.
OKAY, WE'RE GOING TO GO ALL OUT FILMING AGAIN TODAY!
HARU-HI.
I HAVE TO WONDER... WHY DID I SAY THOSE WORDS AT THE TIME?
LET'S ABSOLUTELY MAKE THIS FILM A SUCCESS.

OF COURSE!
I'M THE DIRECTOR, AFTER ALL!!
DON (BOOM)
SUCCESS IS GUARANTEED.
I DON'T NEED YOU TO TELL ME THAT!
MUST HAVE GOTTEN CARRIED AWAY.
I'M PRONE TO AN OVER-ABUNDANCE OF ENTHUSIASM...
(ER, WHO AM I TRYING TO EXPLAIN MYSELF TO?)

OKAY, IS EVERY-BODY READY?

WE'LL BE SHOOTING A BUNCH OF SCENES BY THE RIVER!

AFTER SCHOOL...

GATAN (CLATTER)

ガタ

GATAN

郁陽園

ガタン...

SIGN: KOUYOUEN

NOTH-ING...

PERHAPS YOU COULD TELL ME WHAT YOU SAID FOR FUTURE REFERENCE?

A DEJECTED SUZUMIYA-SAN HAS BECOME AS SUNNY AS THIS AUTUMN SKY...

IMPRES-SIVE.

ARMBAND: SUPER-DIRECTOR

I WAS STARTING TO UNDER-STAND HOW TO DEAL WITH HER.

IT'S BETTER TO GO WITHOUT A PLAN...

I JUST TOLD HER HOW I FELT.

ATTACK HEAD-ON.
IT'S BEST TO DO WHATEVER COMES TO MIND...
パソコン
ATREYU
カレー
BESIDES, WHO WANTED TO BE CREEPED OUT BY A DEJECTED HARUHI?
WOW! AMAZING!
LOOK! THE CHERRY BLOSSOMS ARE IN FULL BLOOM!
I DIDN'T KNOW THIS COULD HAPPEN!
HUH ...?

I WAS JUST THINKING ABOUT HOW I WANTED A SHOT WITH CHERRY BLOSSOMS.
THIS ABNORMAL WEATHER HAS PERFECT TIMING!
HEY... WHAT IS THIS?
I DON'T KNOW.
WE'LL USE THE CHERRY BLOSSOMS AS A BACKDROP FOR THE LAST SCENE!
THE HERO AND HEROINE WILL WALK HAND-IN-HAND DOWN THE TREE-LINED PATH.
HOW CONVENIENT THAT WE ALSO HAVE DOVES HERE!

A COMPLETE FOOL...

I WAS A FOOL.

HM?

HAVE YOU NO-TICED?

THE REST OF US WERE GETTING MORE WRINKLES ON OUR FACES.

HARUHI WAS THE ONLY ONE WHO BELIEVED FILMING WAS GOING WELL.

AND YEAH, THERE YOU HAVE IT.

THEY'RE SUPPOSED TO BE EXTINCT...

THOSE BIRDS... THEY'RE PASSENGER PIGEONS.

BASA
BASA
BASA (FLAP)
EVERYDAY LIFE WAS FALLING APART AROUND US.
BA
BA
H-HOLD ONNN!?
ZUBA (KABLAM)
BA (BLAM)
THE MODEL GUN FIRED WATER BULLETS.
DON (BOOM)
WAUGH...!
THE CONTACT LENS FIRED SOME KIND OF SUPER-WEAPON THAT MODERN SCIENCE COULDN'T EXPLAIN.
SHUTA (SHOONK)
WHICH LED TO ASAHINA-SAN BEING BITTEN BY NAGATO EACH TIME.

OKAY! DO XXX (SOME-THING CRAZY) ...!!
バサァ
BASAA
XXX (SCREW REASONABLE) AND GO XXX (ABSOLUTELY INSANE)!
WAH!? THAT'S INSANE!
ガビン
GABIN (SHOCK)
BUT EVERY-THING THAT BEGINS MUST END.
OR AT THE VERY LEAST, THIS MOVIE MUST...!
YES! OKAY!!
BAN (BAM)
バン!!

GOOD WORK!
KAAAAN (CLAAANG)
WE'RE DONE FILMING NOW.
EVERYBODY WORKED HARD.
ESPE-CIALLY ME.
YEP, I'M AWESOME.
GREAT JOB!
FUNYA (FAINT)
WAH ...
WHAT'S WRONG, MIKURU-CHAN? ARE YOU OVER-COME BY EMOTION?
SAVE YOUR TEARS FOR WHEN YOU'RE AWARDED A PALME D'OR!
......

PUU (HONK)
WAI (CHATTER)
WAI
WE SHOULD PROBABLY SELL THIS TO HOLLYWOOD.
WAI
WAI
I'LL NEED TO SIGN A SKILLED AGENT!
KO (CLACK)
STILL...
...NOW THAT WE'RE FINISHED, IT FEELS LIKE IT WAS OVER IN AN INSTANT.
KO
KO
TIME FLIES WHEN YOU'RE HAVING FUN.
EVERY-BODY'S DISMISSED...!!

WHO WAS HAVING FUN...?

GOOOO (WHOOSH)

ゴ

オ

オ

オ

SORRY.

ORIGINALLY, WE WOULD BE CELEBRATING THE COMPLETION OF THE MOVIE...

KO (CLACK)

コ

WELL...

ASAHINA-SAN... WERE THOSE TEARS OF RELIEF?

BUT IT MAY BE TOO EARLY FOR THAT...

YOU MANAGED TO ESCALATE THE SITUATION.

KO

コ

KO

コ

I WISH YOU HAD SHOWED RESTRAINT WHEN CHEERING HER UP.

I'LL ADMIT THAT I WAS ALSO MISTAKEN.

PURURU (RRRING)

YOU CAN'T READ HER MIND...

I ASSUMED THAT RELIEVING HER STRESS WOULD PREVENT HER "POWER" FROM ACTIVATING.

PURURU

BESIDES, THAT'S ONLY ACCORDING TO YOUR LITTLE THEORY.

YOU CAN'T BE TOO SURE...

SFX: FU (HEH)

I DOUBT I COULD CONVINCE HER TO ACCEPT THAT AT THIS POINT...

THAT IT WAS ALL A DREAM?

WHICH IS WHY...

...ONE MORE PUSH IS NECESSARY...

THE TRUTH IS...
SU (SLIDE)
...MY FACTION AND ASAHINA-SAN'S FACTION ARE NOT THE ONLY ONES FOCUSED ON SUZUMIYA-SAN.
THERE ARE *MANY OTHERS.*
I WOULD LOVE TO GIVE YOU A DIGEST OF THE STRUGGLES GOING ON UNDER THE SURFACE.
A TRULY BLOODY AFFAIR...
ENOUGH OF YOUR CRAZY TALK.
HEH HEH ...
EXCUSE ME.

I DIDN'T NEED TO TELL YOU THAT.
PERHAPS THE FATIGUE IS CATCHING UP TO ME.
I DO NOT BELIEVE THAT OUR THEORY IS ABSOLUTELY CORRECT.
HOWEVER... I MUST ACCEPT IT IN ORDER TO CARRY ON.
NOBODY CAN BREAK FROM THEIR INTENDED ROLE.

NEITHER SUZUMIYA-SAN'S LOVABLE CHARACTER...
...NOR YOU, NATURALLY...
YOU'VE DONE WELL TO COME THIS FAR, KYON.
TIME FOR THE LAST SPRINT!

REALLY *FLASHY* ONES!

VFX...?

WITH *VFX* ADDED IN!

THE DAY BEFORE THE CULTURAL FESTIVAL

WE'RE GOING TO EDIT ALL OF THE FOOTAGE WE HAVE INTO A MOVIE.

AND THE OTHER THREE AREN'T AROUND BECAUSE THEY'RE WORKING ON THEIR CLASS PREPARA- TIONS.

ARE YOU STUPID!? I DON'T HAVE THE SKILLS.

I MEAN, THE CULTURAL FESTIVAL IS TOMORROW ...

I'LL HELP TOO.

ZUI (LOOM)

YOU SHOULD BE ABLE TO FINISH IF YOU STAY OVERNIGHT, RIGHT?

カタ
KATA (CLICK)
カタ
KATA
カタ
KATA
カタ
KATA
カタ
KATA
OH!
CUT OFF A LITTLE FROM THAT SCENE!
EH ...?
SHOULDN'T THAT BE ENOUGH ALREADY ...?
KATA
KATA
KATA
KATA
KATA
KATA
JUST A LITTLE MORE!
KEEP IT UP!
AN EXPRESSION OF GRATITUDE.
FROM BOTH MY ORGANIZATION AND MYSELF...

SO PLEASE FIND A METHOD THAT DOESN'T DRAMATICALLY ALTER THIS WORLD...
THE WORLD WE CURRENTLY LIVE IN IS RATHER NICE.
I'M SURE YOU FEEL THE SAME WAY...!
WE ALSO NEED TO MAKE A STAFF ROLL.
WITH A "FIN" AT THE END...
... HARUHI.
ガタ
GATA (CLATTER)

I HAVE A SUGGES-TION FOR ENDING THIS MOVIE...!
YOU BETTER ACCEPT IT AFTER ALL THE CRAP I'VE PUT UP WITH.

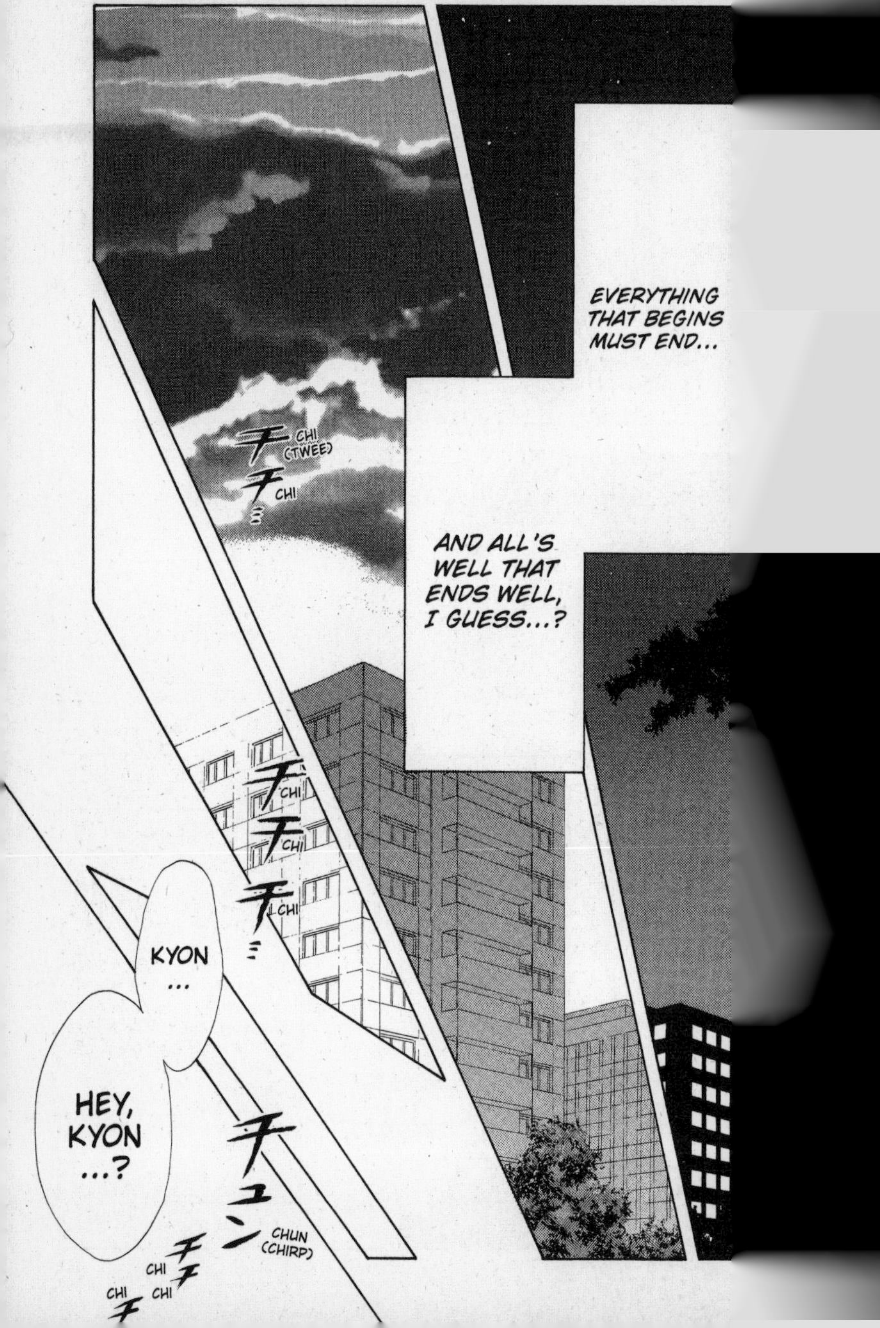
EVERYTHING THAT BEGINS MUST END...
AND ALL'S WELL THAT ENDS WELL, I GUESS...?
チ CHI (TWEE)
チ CHI
チ CHI
チ CHI
チ CHI
KYON...
HEY, KYON...?
チュン CHUN (CHIRP)
チ CHI
チ CHI
チ CHI

HEY, HOW'D IT GO?

FチFチFチ CHI (TWEE) CHI CHI

MM...

ムクッ MUKU (RISE)

FチFチ CHI CHI

......

WHOA.

KACHI (CLICK)

スーー CLICK

WHERE'S THE MOVIE?

THOUGH I WAS SO EXHAUSTED THAT I FELL ASLEEP BEFORE I COULD PULL AN ALL-NIGHTER...

...NOW THAT I THINK ABOUT IT, THIS IS THE FIRST TIME I'VE EVER STAYED OVERNIGHT AT SCHOOL.

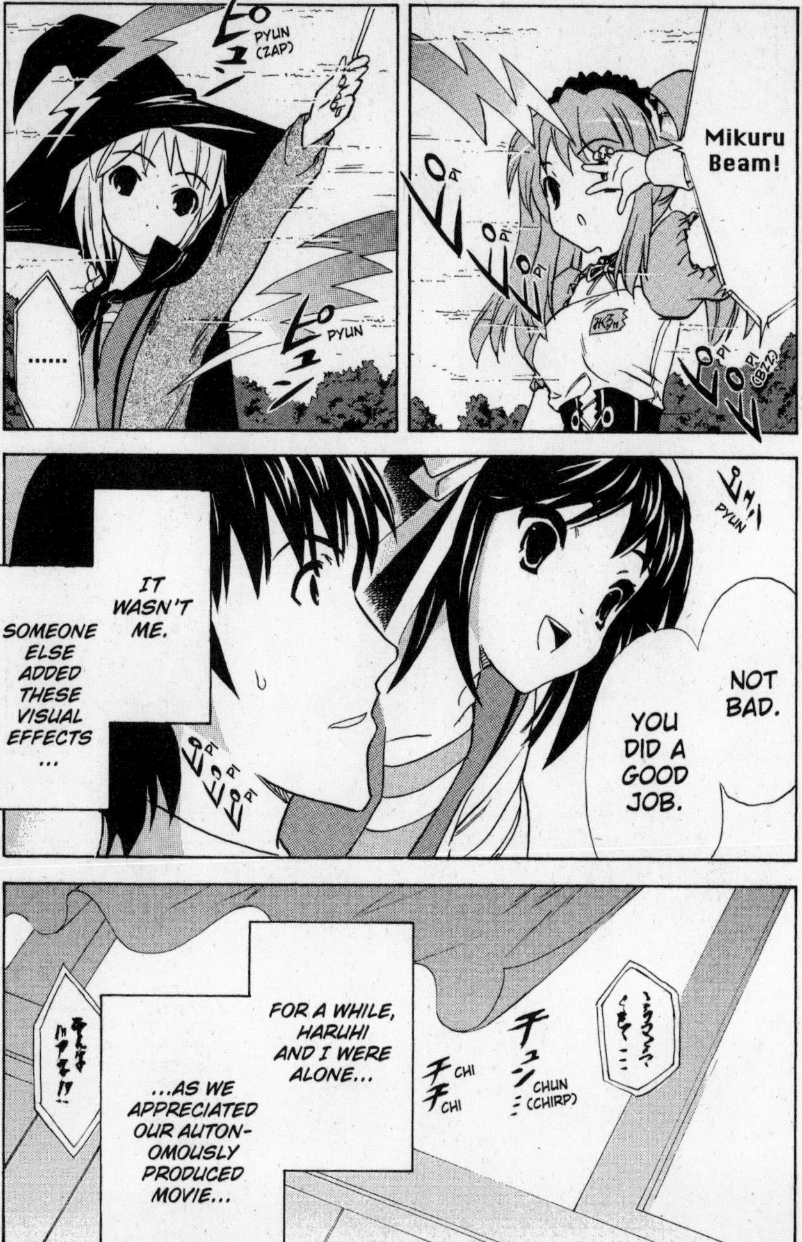
Mikuru Beam!
PI PI PI
PI PI (BZZ)
PYUN (ZAP)
PYUN
......
PYUN
NOT BAD.
YOU DID A GOOD JOB.
IT WASN'T ME.
SOMEONE ELSE ADDED THESE VISUAL EFFECTS...
PI PI PI
CHUN (CHIRP)
CHI CHI
FOR A WHILE, HARUHI AND I WERE ALONE...
...AS WE APPRECIATED OUR AUTONOMOUSLY PRODUCED MOVIE...

...IT'S FUNNY.
THE STORY WAS A TRAIN WRECK AND YOU COULD BARELY HEAR THE LINES.
AND YOU COULD EVEN HEAR THE DIRECTOR YELLING IN THE BACK-GROUND.
BUT WAS IT MY IMAGINATION, OR DID THE EFFECTS, COURTESY OF AN UNKNOWN BENEFACTOR, MAKE THIS MOVIE KIND OF WATCHABLE?
HA HA ...

HAD WE BEEN WATCHING IT ON A BIG SCREEN INSTEAD OF A LITTLE MONITOR...

...I MIGHT HAVE FELT DIFFER-ENTLY.

EVEN HARUHI WAS SILENT FOR ONCE AS SHE WATCHED.

TAN

TAN (OMMO)

たん

TAN

たんたん

TAN

たん

Starring

TA

TAN

たんたん

TA (OAD)

たんた

TAN

たんた

TA

AND THEN... THE ENDING CREDITS.

TAN

TAN

TAN

たんたん たたた

TA

TA

TAN

たん たんた

TAN

たん

TAN

たん た たんた♪

TA

TAN

TA

MY IDEA WAS TO FORCE HARUHI TO DELIVER THIS NARRATION.

CLOSING WORDS FROM THE DIRECTOR HERSELF ...!

みんみんみらくる♪
MI-MI-MIRACLE!
Starring
Mikuru Asahina
Itsuki Koizumi
Yuki Nagato
Mikuru Asahina
Itsuki Koizumi
Yuki Nagato
This story is a work of fiction. There is no relation to any real people, organizations, events, etc.
みっくるんるん♪
MIKURUN-RUN!

みんみんみらくるん♪
MI-MI-MIRACLE!
THE MAGIC WORDS THAT CANCELED OUT EVERYTHING THAT HAD HAPPENED.
みっくるんるん♪
MIKURUN-RUN!
It's all made-up!
HEH HEH ...
I INCLUDED THIS BECAUSE YOU WERE SO INSISTENT ...

But shouldn't it be obvious?
How could such a fantastic story happen in real life?
かもん れっつだんす♪
COME ON, LET'S DANCE!
かもん れっつだんす♪
COME ON, LET'S DANCE!
ALL'S WELL THAT ENDS WELL...
Fin
BAAABY!
べ〜いび〜♪
...IGNORING THE QUALITY OF THE MOVIE ITSELF.

THE SIGH OF HARUHI SUZUMIYA V : END

I WANNA GO! I WANNA GO!
I WANNA GO TO KYON-KUN'S SCHOOL CULTURAL FESTIVAL!
SHOW MUST GO ON
LIKE I ALREADY SAID, NO!
THIS ISN'T LIKE ONE OF YOUR GRADE SCHOOL EVENTS.
BE A GOOD GIRL AND WATCH THE HOUSE FOR US.
BATAN (SLAM)
BOO ...
I HAVE TO GO SEE THIS!

◎ SHOW MUST GO ON

WAI (CHATTER)
北高祭
WAI
SERIOUSLY, THIS MORNING WAS SUCH A PAIN.
I STOPPED BY MY HOUSE TO GET CHANGED AND WAS IMMEDIATELY CAUGHT BY MY SISTER...
SIGN: NORTH HIGH FESTIVAL
WAI
WAI
SIGN: BAZAAR
SIGN: SHOCKING MONSTER WORLD
I WAS TIRED AFTER STAYING UP ALL NIGHT FOR THE MOVIE DIRECTED BY HARUHI.
I'D LIKE TO RELAX TODAY, FOR ONCE...
HEY, KYON-KUN!

WHAT!?
MY SISTER IS HERE!?
YEP! JUST SAW HER.
Y'KNOW HOW OUR CLASS IS DOING A YAKISOBA CAFÉ, RIGHT?
THERE HAPPENED TO BE AN EXTRA MAID OUTFIT THAT WAS SMALL ENOUGH FOR HER.
SHE WAS A HUGE HIT!
わーい
YAY!
I CAME TO THANK YOU...BUT I GUESS YOU DIDN'T KNOW.

A BIG HIT... I'VE GOT A BAD FEELING ABOUT THIS.
WHENEVER THERE'S EXCITEMENT, YOU-KNOW-WHO CAN BE FOUND.
OH, HOW ADORABLE! SINCE YOU'RE HERE, YOU SHOULD ENJOY YOURSELF!
KYON, SHOW HER AROUND!
I CAN SEE THAT HAPPENING.
THOSE CLOTHES ARE ADORABLE! THEN I'LL MOBILIZE THE ENTIRE SOS BRIGADE!
WE'LL GO HELP OUT AT THE CAFÉ RIGHT AWAY!
I CAN DEFINITELY SEE THAT HAPPENING!!
TSURUYA-SAN! WHERE IS MY SISTER RIGHT NOW!?
UMMM... I'M PRETTY SURE THAT...
...SHE'S STILL IN THE MAID OUTFIT, SO SHE SHOULD BE EASY TO SPOT.

SIGN: HAUNTED HOUSE
お化け屋
WAI (CHATTER)
ワイ
KA
カ
KA (CLACK)
カ
THAT'S RIGHT...SHE SEEMED TO GET ALONG WITH HARUHI, ODDLY ENOUGH...
I NEED TO STOP HER BEFORE THIS GETS UGLY.
ワイ
WAI
100円バザー
大人のおもちゃ
OH? WHY HELLO THERE.
POSTER: HAMLET: NEW INTERPRETATION
ハムレット
OH, THAT'S RIGHT.
YOU SAID THAT YOUR CLASS IS DOING A PLAY.
YES, INDEED.
IT WAS DIFFICULT TO MEMORIZE LINES FOR THE PLAY AND THE MOVIE AT THE SAME TIME.

I'M NOT HERE TO SEE THE PLAY.
MY SISTER WAS HERE, RIGHT?
AH! THAT'S WHY YOU'RE HERE.
SORRY, BUT I'M TAKING HER HOME.
I DON'T MIND.
BUT... WILL THAT BE POS-SIBLE?
SHII (SHHH)
WE CAN WATCH FROM OVER HERE.
HUH? STAGE CUR-TAINS ...
!?

......

WHAT IS SHE DOING...

DOGON
(DUUUM)

ONE OF THE ACTORS FORGOT HIS PROP SWORD ON STAGE.

WE WERE TRYING TO DEVISE A WAY TO RETRIEVE IT UNOBTRUSIVELY.

THAT WAS WHEN YOUR SISTER ...

OKAY!? I'M SMALL, SO I CAN GO GET IT!

LET ME DO IT!

BI
(JAB)

MAN...

WHAT'S SHE GRINNING ABOUT?

...BUT NOW SHE'S UNABLE TO MAKE HER WAY BACK.

SHE MANAGED TO SUCCESS-FULLY RETRIEVE THE SWORD...

HEY... GET HER OFF THE STAGE.

NOW!

SO THIS IS A CULTURAL FESTIVAL. SO MUCH CULTURE!

AH, THIS IS SO FUN!

PI (FLICK)

I SEE.

I'LL USE YOUR IDEA.

FUASA (FWAP)

ZAAA

WHAT? THAT'S...

HEY... I'M BOR-ROWING THIS.

BUT... THE LIGHTS WON'T BE DIMMING ANY-TIME SOON.

HIHIIN (WHINNY)

THAT'S ENOUGH!

THIS BRUTAL BEHAVIOR CANNOT BE TOLERATED.

I, GUILDEN-STERN, AND MY BELOVED HORSE EXUPÉRL SHALL NOT STAND FOR THIS!

BAN (BAN)

MY ABILITY TO IMPROVISE HAS IMPROVED, THANKS TO A CERTAIN SOMEONE...

A SPLENDID DISPLAY OF WIT.

AUDIENCE

ACTOR ACTOR

PANELS

WHO IS EXUPÉRL?

I DID SOME THINKING.

WE SIMPLY NEED TO SECURE A ROUTE FOR YOUR SISTER TO REACH THE PANELS ON STAGE.

YOU SAVED ME, KYON-KUN.
WE CAN TALK LATER.
THE PLAY WAS APPARENTLY A CLASSICAL PIECE...
KOTSUN (KNOCK)
...SO A MAID CARRYING A SWORD ...
PATAN (SLAM)
...COULDN'T POSSIBLY BE EX-PLAINED.

OH!? WHERE AM I!?
チャッ!
CHA (SHK)
I'VE BEEN CAUGHT UP IN A DIFFERENT TIME!?
メイド焼きそば
仁王
伝統と革新
お待ちしております
ギョッ
GYO (SHOCK)
WHAT ...!?
PAPER: MAID YAKISOBA CAFE, DOUBLE DEVA, TRADITION AND INNOVATION AWAIT
A CRUEL TWIST IN SPACE-TIME!?
NO MATTER! ANY WHO STAND IN MY WAY...
!
BASHI (SHING)

...WILL BE CUT DOWN!
MAN ...
...SHE'S GOT BALLS, CONSIDERING SHE'S MY SISTER.
THIS IS THE SECRET SWORD FROM THE WEST!?
DON'T GO ALONG WITH HER...
DOSA (THUMP)
AUGH...
I'M TAKING THIS HORSE!
WHAT!?

WAAAAIT!
DO
DO
DO (THMP)
DO
I SEE ...
JYAAAN (TA-DAA)
PACHI (CLAP)
PACHI
OO (WHOO)
PACHI
PACHI
OOO
PACHI
JIRIRIRI (CRACKLE)
RIRIRI

パチ PACHI
パチ PACHI
THANK YOU FOR WATCHING!
パチ PACHI
パチ PACHI
パチ PACHI
HEY... WAS THAT REALLY OKAY?
パチ PACHI
パチ PACHI
パチ PACHI
パチ PACHI
IT CERTAINLY WASN'T A FAILURE, BY ANY MEANS.
AND IT WAS GREAT PUBLICITY FOR OUR CAFÉ!
パチ PACHI
THIS IS BUT A CULTURAL FESTIVAL... A SIMPLE "CARNIVAL" AT ITS CORE.
YOU COULD SAY WE TOOK THE MOST APPROPRIATE COURSE OF ACTION FOR AN EVENT SUCH AS A FESTIVAL.
I WAS ALSO CAUGHT UP IN THE ACTION.
THERE YOU HAVE IT!
ゴン GON (WHACK)
DON'T GET TOO COCKY.

OKAY, LET'S GO WORK AT THE CAFÉ AGAIN!
AYE AYE, SIR!
MEH ... I WAS GOING TO YELL AT HER A LITTLE MORE.
IT'S IMPOS-SIBLE TO OVERCOME CRYING CHILDREN AND PEOPLE WHO ARE HAVING FUN...
... SHOULDN'T YOU BE AWARE OF THAT?
I THINK... I'VE FIGURED OUT WHY SHE AND HARUHI GET ALONG SO WELL.
IN ANY CASE, YOUR ACTING WASN'T TOO SHABBY.
UP FOR THE AFTER-NOON SHOW?
I'LL PASS.
ANY MORE HARD LABOR AND I'LL REALLY BE A CART HORSE...

Show Must Go On : END

THE NUMBER OF PEOPLE WHO CAME TO WATCH WAS SURPRISING, THOUGH I GUESS IT REALLY WASN'T.

THE MOVIE WAS A DECENT SUCCESS, THANKS TO FANS OF ASAHINA-SAN.

GYAGYAN (KABOOM)

PI (BZZ)

PI

PI

PI

AND SO, THE FILMING OF THE SURREALIST MOVIE WAS FINALLY OVER WITH.

LIVE : A LIVE

SO THE MEMBERS OF THE SOS BRIGADE WERE ENJOYING THIS CULTURAL FESTIVAL SEPARATELY.

FORTUNATELY, HARUHI HAD TAKEN THE INITIATIVE IN HANDLING NEGOTIATIONS AND PROMOTION.

COUPON: MAID YAKISOBA CAFÉ, DOUBLE DEVA, 200 YEN OFF, COME ON TOPKNOT, NORTH HIGH FESTIVAL COMMITTEE

メイド焼きそば

仁王

200円割引

PI (FLIP)

WELL, THERE'S ONE BIT OF BUSINESS THAT I HAVE TO TAKE CARE OF.

AND SO, IT WAS FINALLY THE LAST DAY OF THE CULTURAL FESTIVAL...

GYA (CHATTER)

GYA

FLYERS: SOS BRIGADE PRESENTS "THE ADVENTURES OF MIKURU ASAHINA EPISODE 00"

BUT FIRST ...
...I WONDER HOW THE SOS BRIGADE'S STAR ACTRESS(?) IS DOING.

YOU WILL FINISH EATING IN 4 MINUTES AND 35 SECONDS... DURING THAT TIME, YOU WILL TRAVERSE A TOTAL DISTANCE OF 235 METERS INCLUDING 34 STEPS.

IN 5 MINUTES AND 23 SECONDS, YOU WILL BUY A HOT DOG AND DEPART 16 SECONDS LATER.

FIRST, YOU WILL SPEND 17 MINUTES AND 7 SECONDS AT CLASS 1-E, THEN 5 MINUTES AND 41 SECONDS AT CLASS 2-F, 41 MINUTES AND 35 SECONDS AT CLASS 2-D...

YOU WILL DEPART THIS STRUCTURE IN 2 HOURS AND 30 MINUTES AFTER VISITING FOUR ADDITIONAL ATTRACTIONS.

I HEARD THAT SHE'S SO ACCURATE IT'S SCARY.

...WELL, I EXPECTED AS MUCH.

DON'T GET CARRIED AWAY, NAGATO.

POSTERS: "NEW HAMLET"

1-
新説
ハムレット
上演
9:00~10:10
10:40~11:50
13:00~14:10
14:40~15:50
AS FOR KOIZUMI'S CLASS...I PROBABLY DON'T NEED TO GO.
FROM THE BIT I SAW, OR NO...THE BIT I WAS IN, IT DIDN'T SEEM TO BE MY KIND OF THING.
I HEARD THAT HIS LOOKS WERE HELPING THE PLAY ATTRACT AN AUDIENCE...
WELL, NOT THAT I GIVE A DAMN.
I WAS UTTERLY FOOLED.
TODAY'S MAIN EVENT WAS SOMEWHERE ELSE.
LET'S GO, KYON. TO OUR EDEN.
TO THE COSTUME CAFE FEATURING ASAHINA-SAN AND COMPANY!
...I WOULD HAVE PREFERRED TO ENJOY THIS ALONE IN PEACE.

STILL, I ACTED IN YOUR MOVIE AND EVEN TOOK A DIVE INTO THE WATER...
...AND MY ONLY COMPENSATION IS THIS COUPON? DOESN'T SEEM FAIR.
DON'T COME IF YOU DON'T LIKE IT! GET LOST.
I CAN'T WAIT.
WILL SHE BE IN THAT MINISKIRT OUTFIT LIKE IN THE MOVIE?
DON'T LUMP THIS WITH HARUHI'S VULGAR TASTE.
HEEEEY!
げっ...
GEH...
YOOHOO-!
OVER HERE!

THIS IS ONE HECK OF A LINE.
BUSINESS IS GOOD, HUH?
NYA-HA-HA! THEY REALLY TOOK THE BAIT!
SIGN: 2-2 YAKISOBA CAFÉ
MUUN (HMM)
2-2 焼そば喫茶
I WAS WONDERING WHY THERE WERE ONLY GUYS IN LINE...
...BUT THE REASON WAS PRETTY OBVIOUS.
HOW DO YOU LIKE THE OUTFIT? DON'T YOU THINK IT LOOKS MEGA-GOOD ON ME?
WELL, NYORO?
YOU BET...
NYORO?
WE ONLY HAVE YAKISOBA AND WATER ON THE MENU!
YOU'LL HAVE TO WAIT A LITTLE BIT!

SIGNS: NO PICTURES ALLOWED, WATER IS FREE, 300 YEN YAKISOBA

OKAY! THREE WATERS OVER HERE!
三百円 焼きそば
お水 無料
AFTER WAITING FOR ALMOST THIRTY MINUTES, WE WERE FINALLY SHOWN TO OUR SEATS.
AH, WEL-COME.
大盛りうけたまわります
おおお
OOOH!
THIS IS IT!
UM... WHAT WILL YOU HAVE?
YAKI-SOBA!
OKAY ...
SHE HAS A DIFFERENT RADIANCE FROM WHEN SHE'S IN THE CLUB-ROOM.
SHE LOOKS GREAT IN THAT TASTE-FUL OUTFIT ...

MIKURU'S IN CHARGE OF COLLECTING TICKETS.
I SEE ...
写真撮影は
ご遠慮
下さい!!!
SIGN: PLEASE REFRAIN FROM TAKING PICTURES!!! NO ASKING FOR POSING.
THERE'D BE A HUGE MESS IF YOU LET PEOPLE TAKE PICTURES.
IF WE LET HER CARRY YAKISOBA, SHE MIGHT TRIP AND DROP IT ALL!
A WISE DECISION.
WAITRESS, OVER HERE...
GOTCHA!
SIGNS: FREE WATER, SUPER YUMMY
SIGN: YAKISOBA 300 YEN
THEN I'LL SEE YOU LATER!
YES... HMM?
HEY... ISN'T THAT A PAMPHLET FOR OUR MOVIE?
ASAHINA-SAN... MAGNIFICENT.
THIS HAS TURNED INTO A FAN CLUB GATHERING.
PAMPHLET: "THE ADVENTURES OF MIKURU ASAHINA EPISODE 00" SOS BRIGADE

KARAN (CLINK)
IN THE END, WE WERE QUICKLY CHASED OUT BY NEW CUSTOMERS...
...AND LEFT THE CAFÉ AFTER FINISHING OUR YAKISOBA IN FIVE MINUTES.
THREE LEAVING!
OOF...
I DIDN'T EXPECT THE MAIN EVENT TO END SO SOON...
I WANTED TO SIT DOWN A LITTLE LONGER...
GO
OKAY, GUYS. YOU READY?
LET'S PICK UP GIRLS!
WE'RE TARGETING GROUPS OF THREE OR MORE!
GO BY YOURSELF.
I'LL ALSO PASS.
WHA!?

根性なし
どもがあ〜

SPINELESS WIMPS!

...WELL, WHERE TO NOW?

SIGN: ACCURATE FORTUNE-TELLING

ガヤ (CHATTER)

ガヤ GYA

THOUGH TO BE HONEST, I'M STILL TIRED FROM FILMING THE MOVIE...

...SO I'D PREFER A PLACE WHERE I CAN SIT BACK AND RELAX...

WELL...

吹奏学部
コンサート

講堂

有志バンド

I SHOULD BE ABLE TO SIT DOWN AT LEAST.

PAMPHLET: AMATEUR BANDS, WIND ENSEMBLE CONCERT "DREAMING AND AWAKENING"

北高祭 THE LIVE
パ
PA
(CHONK)
パッ
PA
パッパ
PA
パラッ
PARA
(TOOT)
パ
PA
パッパ
PA
THIS PLACE IS ABOUT SIXTY PERCENT FULL, HUH...
THEY AREN'T AS SERIOUS AS THE ACTORS IN THE PLAY.
NOT A BAD WAY TO RELAX.
ゴク
GOKU
(GULP)

Here is the next band.
Pearl
カチャ
KACHA (CLACK)
BFFT!
ガ
GA (WHAM)
WH-WHAT'S GOING ON?
1...
2...
...

SUZUMIYA-SAN IS QUITE GOOD.
NAGATO-SAN AS WELL, OF COURSE.
KYU (SLIDE)
WHEN DID YOU...
AAAAN (TWANG)

Um, every-body.
I'm supposed to introduce the members now...
SIGN: NORTH HIGH FESTIVAL
Actually, Yuki, over on guitar, and I aren't official members.
Ah, the other two are real members.
We're stand-ins.
So there you have it. I apologize if my performance is shaky.
I only had an hour to practice, so we're kind of winging this.
AREN'T THERE... MORE PEOPLE IN THE AUDIENCE NOW?

If you want to hear these songs performed by the actual members, you can bring a tape to get a copy dubbed?

Oh, that's it!

NI (GRIN)

It's settled then.

SHE'S...

SFX: GU (THUMBS-UP)

WAAAAA (CHEER)

Then here's the last song!

WAAAAA
IS THIS REALLY THAT EXCITING...?
THIS INTENSITY ISN'T BECAUSE THE CULTURAL FESTIVAL IS ALMOST OVER.
TON (TAP) TON TON TON
AAAA
NAGATO ASIDE... HARUHI'S PERFORMANCE WAS CERTAINLY IMPRESSIVE.

VE

THE AUDIENCE WAS GOING CRAZY OVER A BAND COBBLED TOGETHER ON THE SPOT.
AS I STOOD THERE... I COULD FEEL THE CULTURAL FESTIVAL COME TO AN END.
WAAAAAAAAAAA (CHEEEEER)

"A MOVIE IS ONLY FICTION."
WE WERE ABLE TO CLEAN UP THE MOVIE MESS BY MAKING HARUHI UNDERSTAND THAT.
HOWEVER, THIS REALITY COULDN'T BE WRITTEN OFF AS FICTION.
HARUHI AND I... AND THE OTHER MEMBERS OF THE SOS BRIGADE WERE STILL HERE.
YOU COULDN'T SAY THAT "WE DIDN'T EXIST."

KYURARARARARA (WAAAAAIL)
WE MAY EVENTUALLY GO OUR SEPARATE WAYS...
...BUT FOR NOW, WE WERE EXPERIENCING HIGH SCHOOL LIFE TOGETHER.
SINCE THE WORLD STILL EXISTS.
OR AS NAGATO WOULD PUT IT...
..."FOR ME, AT LEAST."
THANK YOU, EVERY-ONE!

SIGN: NORTH HIGH FESTIVAL

OOOOOO (WHOOOOO)
北高祭 THE LIV
AND SO, I NEVER GOT A CHANCE TO RELAX ...
...AS OUR CULTURAL FESTIVAL CAME TO A CLOSE.

THAT DAY... I WAS HEADED BACK TO THE CLUB-ROOM...
...WHEN I SAW THE BAND ARGUING ABOUT WHETHER THEY WERE GOING TO TAKE THE STAGE.
THE GIRL ON GUITAR AND VOCALS HAD A HIGH FEVER AND TONSILLITIS.
IT'S THEIR LAST NORTH HIGH FESTIVAL, SO SHE WAS SET ON PERFORMING, EVEN IF IT KILLED HER.
THEY'D WRITTEN SONGS AND PRACTICED HARD FOR THIS.
IT'D BE ONE THING IF SHE DID EVERYTHING ALONE, BUT THE OTHER MEMBERS' HARD WORK WOULD ALSO HAVE GONE TO WASTE...
DON'T WANT THAT, RIGHT?
THAT'S WHERE YOU CAME IN?

STILL, WHEN DID YUKI LEARN HOW TO PLAY GUITAR?

I HAD TO FRANTICALLY LEARN THE SONGS IN AN HOUR...

THAT WAS WHEN THE HARD PART BEGAN.

YES... YOU MIGHT BE ABLE TO PULL IT OFF.

THERE ARE VISITORS FOR SUZUMIYA-SAN.

PROBABLY HAPPENED THE SECOND YOU ASKED HER.

HEY THERE.

...COME WITH ME.

GO ON.

......

IS YOUR TONSILLITIS CURED?
YES... FOR THE MOST PART.
IT'S INCREDIBLE! WE'VE HAD A FLOOD OF FANS DROP BY.
AND WE'VE DUBBED JUST AS MANY COPIES!
I SEE... THAT'S WONDER-FUL.
WE'RE IN YOUR DEBT.
IT WAS ALL YOUR DOING.
THANK YOU, SUZUMIYA-SAN.

I WISH WE COULD SHOW OUR APPRECIATION...
IT'S OKAY, IT'S OKAY.
I ENJOYED SINGING... AND THEY WERE GOOD SONGS.
I'D FEEL GUILTY IF YOU DID ANYTHING.
IN THAT CASE, THEN...
...YOU'RE MORE THAN WELCOME TO COME TO OUR CONCERTS.
YES, WITH YOUR...
...FRIEND, IF YOU LIKE.
...SURE.
...HARUHI HAD A STRAINED LOOK ON HER FACE THE ENTIRE TIME.

Did you notice how Suzumiya-san's singing was slightly off-rhythm?
There was a lingering impression on the audience...
At an un-conscious level, naturally.
It planted the notion...
...that a performance by the original members must be spectacular ...
SERI-OUSLY... I DIDN'T ASK FOR AN EXPLANA-TION.
PUCHI (CLICK)

SARA (RUSTLE)
SARA
YO.
SARA
YOU'VE HAD A FUNNY LOOK ON YOUR FACE THIS WHOLE TIME.
SARA
SARA
SOME-THING ON YOUR MIND?
MMM... I CAN'T SEEM TO CALM DOWN.
WAS THAT GOOD ENOUGH?

TO BE HONEST, I THINK YOU DID FINE.
HARUHI, YOU'RE FEELING THIS WAY...
...BECAUSE YOU AREN'T USED TO BEING APPRE-CIATED BY OTHER PEOPLE.
YOU'RE ALWAYS DOING THINGS THAT WOULDN'T WARRANT A THANK-YOU.
IT WAS THE SAME DURING THE ATHLETIC FESTIVAL.
HAVE YOU WARMED UP TO THE IDEA OF DOING GOOD DEEDS?
HEH HEH...
WHAT!?
BUT... YEAH.
IT WAS FUN.

HOW SHOULD I PUT IT?
I'M STARTING TO QUESTION WHAT I'M DOING WITH MY LIFE.
THAT'S GOOD.
SHIN (SILENCE)
HM?
CAN YOU PLAY AN INSTRUMENT?
NO.

LET'S MAKE A BAND TO PLAY IN NEXT YEAR'S CULTURAL FESTIVAL.
IT SHOULD BE A CINCH FOR US!
SUKU (RISE)
I'LL HANDLE VOCALS AND YUKI CAN PLAY GUITAR.
WE CAN GIVE MIKURU-CHAN A TAMBOURINE TO HOLD OR SOMETHING.
OF COURSE, WE HAVE TO FILM THE SEQUEL TO OUR MOVIE.
WE'LL BE BUSY NEXT YEAR!
GEH...
GU (GRAB)
HERE WE GO AGAIN?
WE DON'T HAVE TIME TO STAND AROUND.
TA (DASH)
WE NEED TO PLAN EVERYTHING OUT RIGHT AWAY!

HEY! ISN'T IT A LITTLE EARLY?
WHAT ARE YOU TALKING ABOUT? WE HAVE SO MANY THINGS TO DO!
SA (WHOOSH)
SA
SA
C'MON! WALK BY YOURSELF!
WE'RE TAKING THE STEPS THREE AT A TIME!
I HAD NO CHOICE BUT TO RUN WITH HER.
SINCE HARUHI'S HAND WOULDN'T BE RELEASING MINE FOR THE TIME BEING.
LIVE A LIVE : END

IT WAS AN AUTUMN DAY AFTER THE EXCITEMENT OF THE CULTURAL FESTIVAL HAD WORN OFF.
EVERYBODY WORKED HARD DURING THE CULTURAL FESTIVAL.
WELL? HOW ABOUT GOING ON A PICNIC TO WIND DOWN?
PAID FOR OUT OF THE BRIGADE CHIEF'S POCKET?
WHO SAID ANYTHING ABOUT THAT?
JUST ASKING.
SARA (RUSTLE)
SARA

Tales From The Thousand Lakes

AND SO, ON SUNDAY ...
...WE RODE THE TRAIN FOR ABOUT AN HOUR TO ARRIVE AT A SMALL LAKE.
TRAIN: REGULAR
普通
GOO (ROAR)

SOON AFTER, WE REACHED THE PICNICKING TRAIL.
THERE WERE FAMILIES AND COUPLES ENJOYING THEM-SELVES...
I SEE. A PERFECT PLACE FOR TAKING A STROLL.
ISN'T THIS PLACE GREAT?
INDEED.
THE AIR IS SO PURE, CONSIDERING HOW WE AREN'T VERY FAR FROM THE CITY.

THE TRAIL APPEARS TO GO IN A 'V' AROUND THE TWO LAKES.
SHOULD BE OVER IN NO TIME.
DON'T RELAX YET.
THERE'S SUPPOSED TO BE A WATER GOD IN THIS LAKE!
PI (POINT) ぴ
HUH?
LOOK, THEY'RE RENTING OUT PRIESTESS OUTFITS.
貸衣装有ります
...THEY PROBABLY USED TO PERFORM RITUALS IN THOSE OUTFITS.
NOW IT'S JUST A TOURISM SPOT.
巫女
OKAY, LET'S HEAD OUT!

SIGN: COSTUMES FOR RENT

チ CHI (TWEE)
チ CHI
チ CHI
CHI チ
CHI チ
WHAT A MAGNIFICENT VIEW!
IT'S TRULY MARVELOUS.
I NEVER REALIZED THERE WAS SUCH A PLACE NEARBY.
WELL, I HAVE TO CONCUR WITH THAT SENTIMENT.
THIS IS PRETTY GOOD FOR A PLACE THAT'S ONLY AN HOUR AWAY.
BUT A WATER GOD, HUH...

竜神の

深50メートルまでは豊富

シウム等を含んでおりま

生時代の趣を残す集落

れています。

バナジウム イオン	
マンガン	
カリウム	
ナトリウ	

I'M PRETTY
SURE THAT
HARUHI
DOESN'T
BELIEVE IN
THAT CRAP.

STILL,
ALL THAT
HISTORY'S
BEEN
TURNED INTO
A HIKING
COURSE
NOW.

WE'RE
ALMOST
HALFWAY
THROUGH.

THIS
IS WHAT
YOU GET
WITH A
PICNICKING
TRAIL.

I DIDN'T
EXPECT
THE PATH
TO BE SO
FLAT...

HUH? WE
ALREADY
CIRCLED
AROUND
ONCE?

LET'S TRY ON THOSE PRIESTESS OUTFITS.

IT'S A TOUR FOR RECEIVING AN ORACLE FROM THE WATER GOD!

I'M GOING TO END UP WITH INDIGESTION, AT THIS RATE...

SIGN: COSTUMES CAN BE RENTED AT THE RATE OF ¥500 PER HOUR, WE OFFER PRIESTESS OUTFITS IN ALL SIZES

YOU REALLY JUST WANT TO TAKE PICTURES AS SOUVENIRS, DON'T YOU...

¥500 TO RENT ONE FOR AN HOUR!

I KNEW THIS WAS COMING...

BUT STILL, I WAS A LITTLE INTERESTED IN SEEING ASAHINA-SAN IN A PRIESTESS OUTFIT...

AND SO...

THE WORLD IS SUCH A CONVENIENT PLACE NOW!

THE WATER GOD IS PROBABLY SIGHING IN DESPAIR.

WHY NOT? WE HAVE MORE THAN ENOUGH TIME.

SORRY TO KEEP YOU WAITING!

JYAN (TADA)

NOT MUCH FOR ME TO SAY.

THIS TRIO OF GIRLS WOULD LOOK GOOD IN ANYTHING...

VERY CUTE, VERY CUTE!

H-HOW DO I LOOK ...?

UM... EXCUSE ME.

CUT THAT OUT.

BASAA (RUSTLE)

NAM!

IS THAT RIGHT?

STILL, DOES THIS FEEL LIKE COSPLAY BECAUSE OF HER NORMAL BEHAVIOR?

YOU MUST BE PRIESTESSES AT THIS LAKE.
HUH?
ぺこり
PEKORI (BOW)
I HAVE A FAVOR TO ASK OF YOU. PLEASE HEAR ME OUT.
A STRANGE GIRL STARTED TALKING TO US.
I GUESS THAT SHOWS HOW GENUINE THEY LOOKED...
VERY WELL. GO RIGHT ON AHEAD.
MY LITTLE BROTHER ...
MY LITTLE BROTHER DISAPPEARED!

WE CAME TO HIKE TOGETHER.
BUT WE GOT SEPARATED SOMEHOW WHEN WE REACHED THE LAKE ON THE OTHER SIDE...
THAT'S *REALLY* BAD.
DON'T SAY ANYTHING TO MAKE HER WORRY.
HE MIGHT HAVE BEEN **SPIRITED AWAY.**
I CAN'T FIND HIM BY MYSELF... PLEASE HELP.
BASA (RUSTLE)
SHE LOOKS LIKE SHE'S IN SECOND OR THIRD GRADE? PRECOCIOUS KID...
SHE'S BEHAVING VERY RESPONSIBLY FOR HER AGE.
ONE THING, THOUGH... I'M PRETTY SURE IT WAS A MISTAKE TO COME TO THIS GIRL.
LEAVE IT TO ME!

UNDERSTAND? THIS IS A TRIAL FROM THE WATER GOD.
IN OTHER WORDS, YOUR FAITH IS BEING TESTED... DON'T WORRY.
WE WILL BE RESPONSIBLE FOR PRAYING.
I'M SURE THAT YOUR BROTHER WILL BE RETURNED.
CAN'T BELIEVE THAT SHE CAN COME UP WITH LIES LIKE THAT ON THE SPOT.
ぐえ
GUE (YANK)
HOLD ON. WE NEED TO HAVE A LITTLE MEETING.
DON'T GROW UP TO BE LIKE HER.
HURRY IT UP!

SO... WHAT DO WE DO?
THAT'S OBVIOUS. WE GO LOOK FOR HER BROTHER.
I'LL GO TELL THEM TO BROAD-CAST THAT THERE'S A MISSING CHILD.
WHAT ARE YOU TALKING ABOUT? THAT'S OUT OF THE QUES-TION.
THERE WOULDN'T BE ANY DREAMS OR HOPE THAT WAY.
THEN HOW DO WE DO THIS?
DREAMS...?
YES...
THIS TOURIST SPOT IS FAIRLY LARGE...

FIRST, HARUHI AND ASAHINA-SAN WOULD POSE AS IF THEY WERE PRAYING TO THE WATER GOD.

MEANWHILE, THE REST OF THE MEMBERS WOULD FIND THE LOST CHILD...

SHA (SWISH)

THIS WAS HARUHI'S IDEA.

YOOO (WAIL)

AND THE OPERATION BEGINS...I SUPPOSE.

SHA

SHA

"DON'T DO ANYTHING TO RUIN THE DREAMS OF A CHILD.

"MAKE SURE YOU CONTINUE THE ACT WHEN THE BROTHER RETURNS."

STILL... THIS HIKING COURSE MIGHT NOT BE ANYTHING SPECIAL, BUT IT STRETCHES FIVE KILOMETERS IN EVERY DIRECTION...
THIS IS GOING TO TAKE SOME EFFORT.

BOARD: WEST LAKE, EAST LAKE

"I DON'T WANT TO RUIN THE DREAMS OF A CHILD..."
IT'S NOT THAT I DON'T UNDERSTAND HARUHI'S SENTIMENT.
I'D LIKE TO MAKE THIS WORK... WELL NOW.
... THERE.
HM?
NAGATO-SAN, IS SOMETHING WRONG?

...A BOOK BAG.
WHAT'S GOING ON?
THERE'S A NAME TAG.
DOES IT MATCH?
...I'VE GOT A BAD FEELING ABOUT THIS.
THOUGH I DON'T BELIEVE IN THE IDEA OF PEOPLE BEING SPIRITED AWAY.
DID HARUHI WISH FOR SOMEONE TO BE SPIRITED AWAY?
...LIKE, "IT'D BE FUN IF SOMEONE WERE TO BE CURSED"?
WHEN YOU LOOK AT IT THAT WAY, SHE'S PRETTY SCARY...

WE SHALL PROCEED AS FOLLOWS.
I'LL GO SEARCH THE AREA AROUND THE OTHER LAKE FIRST...
YOU AND NAGATO-SAN WILL SEARCH THE LAKE ITSELF.
THE LAKE?
YOU CAN RENT A BOAT.
WORST-CASE SCENARIO?
I DON'T WANT TO CONSIDER THE POSSIBILITY.
BUT TO BE SAFE... YOU'LL HAVE A BETTER VIEW FROM THE SURFACE OF THE LAKE.

WE'VE GOTTEN OURSELVES INTO A REAL MESS...
I'LL LET YOU KNOW IF ANYTHING COMES UP.
TRY TO STAY WITHIN RECEIVING RANGE.
ROGER THAT... YEAH.
...MAN, WE CAN SEE HER FROM THE OTHER SIDE OF THE LAKE.
SHE ATTRACTS A CROWD WHEREVER SHE GOES.
A VI RA HUM KHAM ...!
RETURN HER LITTLE BROTHER ...!
SFX: SHAN (SHAKE) SHAN SHAN
H-HAVE THEY FOUND HIM YET...?
WELL, THEY'LL FIND A WAY TO PULL IT OFF?
...HM?

FOG...?
THIS HAPPENS THE SECOND WE SET SAIL!?
AND THIS FOG IS THICK...
HEY, YOU THERE, NAGATO?
...I AM.
CAN YOU FIND THE KID?
...HE IS PRESENTLY NOT IN THIS SPACE-TIME.

UN- KNOWN ...

WHAT DO YOU MEAN?

!?

THE TERRAIN UNDER- GROUND REMAINS A MYSTERY...

THE TWO LAKES APPEAR TO BE CONNECTED UNDER- GROUND.

HE PRESENTLY ISN'T IN THIS SPACE- TIME? UNKNOWN?

NOT EVEN NAGATO KNOWS...?

PHONE: KOIZUMI: PLEASE TURN BACK IMMEDIATELY.

！

古泉

すぐに引き返して下さい

返信

メニュー

PURURURU (BZZZ)

COULD THIS BE... RELATED TO THE MYSTERY OF THE LAKE?

PLEASE ACCEPT THESE FLOWERS... AND RETURN HER LITTLE BROTHER.

WATER GOD, THIS IS OUR LAST REQUEST...

LIKE THEY SAY, ONLY GOD KNOWS.

ZAWA (MURMUR)

ZAWA

AN HOUR AND A HALF HAS PASSED SINCE THEY BEGAN SEARCHING.

IT MUST HAVE BEEN IMPOSSIBLE...

AHCHOO!

HEY, WHAT'S THAT!?
LOOK OVER THERE!
THE LAKE IS GLOWING!?
WHA ..!?
COULD IT BE...
...THE WATER GOD ...!?
GUO (BOOM)

KA (FLASH)
......
......
HEEEY!
AH...

BIG SIIIS!
WAAA (CHEER)
AAAAA
A
... GUESS WE MADE IT IN TIME.
... HEH.
A
AA
GOOD JOB, KYON.

THANK YOU SO MUCH!!
SORRY ABOUT CAUSING SO MUCH TROUBLE.
PEKORI (BOW)
ぺこり
HE'S SO CUTE.
IT'S FINE. I'M GLAD WE WERE ABLE TO FIND YOU.
BUT...YOU REALLY DON'T REMEMBER ANYTHING?
NUH-UH... WHEN I WOKE UP, I WAS ON THE BOAT.
IT MUST HAVE BEEN THE WATER GOD! I'M SURE OF IT!

THANK YOU VERY MUUUCH!
THOSE KIDS WERE SO POLITE.
I'M REALLY GLAD WE CAME.
THOUGH I WISH I COULD HAVE CHATTED WITH THE WATER GOD...
DON'T BE RIDICULOUS.
UM...I'D LIKE TO CHANGE SOON.
THESE CLOTHES ARE ALL SOAKED FROM THE FOG...
YEAH, YEAH. I KNOW.
SEXY...
THEN ONE LAST TIME.

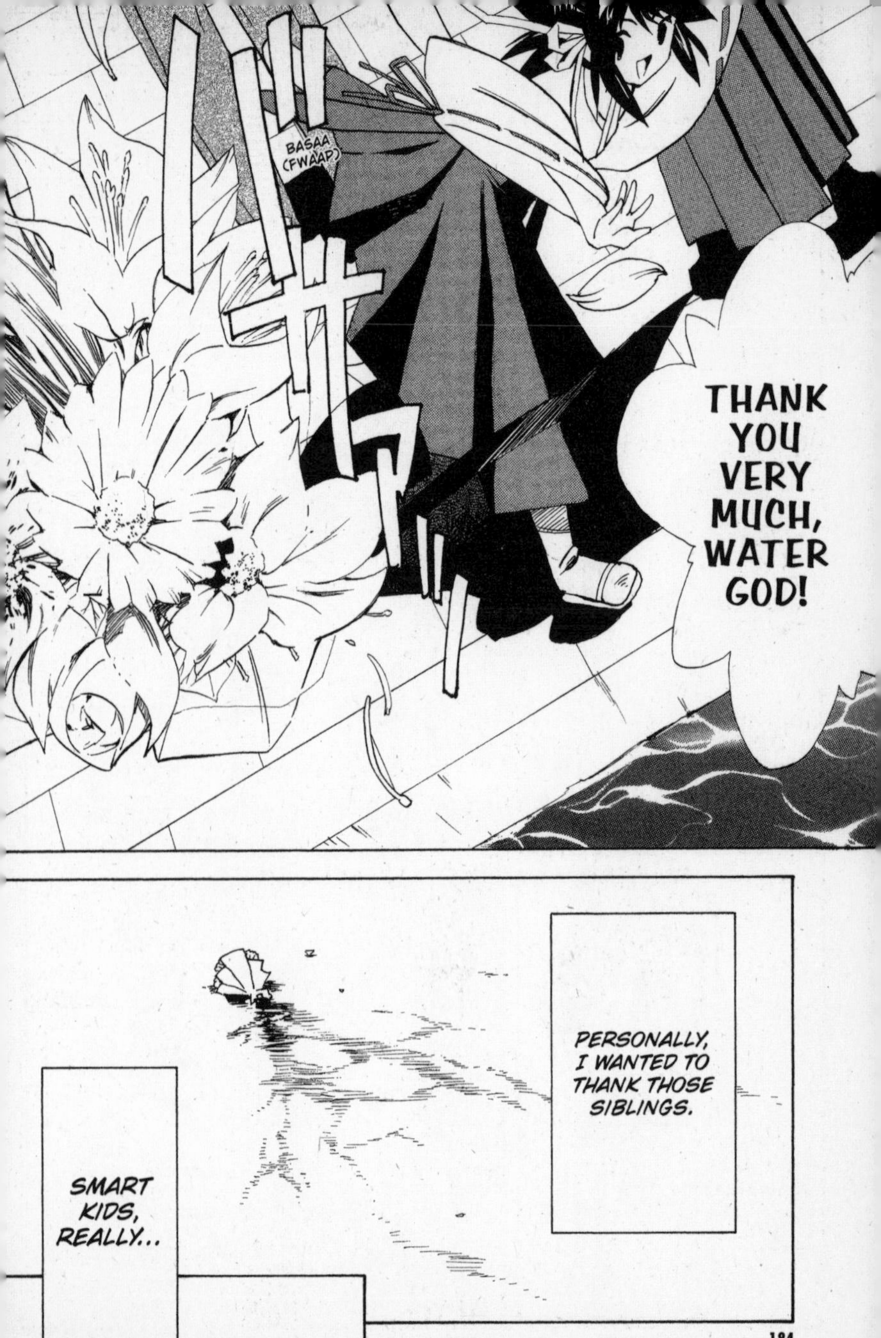
THANK YOU VERY MUCH, WATER GOD!
BASAA (FWAAP)
PERSONALLY, I WANTED TO THANK THOSE SIBLINGS.
SMART KIDS, REALLY...

KOIZUMI FOUND THE LOST BROTHER ON THE LAKE SHORE.
THEN WE PUT HIM IN THE BOAT AS PLANNED...
...AND HAD HIM LIE SO HIS SISTER'S DREAMS WOULDN'T BE RUINED.
WHEN I WOKE UP, I WAS ON THE BOAT ...
HUH ...?
THERE WAS ONE THING I DIDN'T UNDER-STAND.
WHAT WAS WITH THE SHADOW OF A DRAGON?
HEH HEH... SHADOW OF A DRAGON ?
HAVE YOU BEEN INFLUENCED BY THAT GIRL?

WHDA!

WHEN IT EXITED THROUGH THE SURFACE OF THE OTHER LAKE IN AN UNEVEN FASHION, THE FOG SCREEN CREATED THE PROJECTION OF A LIVING CREATURE...

LIGHT WAS DIFFUSED WITHIN THE LAKE THAT WAS EXPOSED TO THE SUN.

IT WAS A COMPLETELY NATURAL PHENOMENON.

WELL... IT MAKES SENSE AFTER YOUR EXPLANATION.

OBVIOUSLY, MY MIND'S ON THE SAME LEVEL AS A CAVEMAN.

PEOPLE IN ANCIENT TIMES PROBABLY BELIEVED IT WAS THE WATER GOD...

BUT STILL.

CERTAINLY A RARE PHENOMENON.

IT PROVIDED FOR A SPECTACULAR SCENE.

THAT HELPS TO ADD AN ELEMENT OF MYSTERY.

THERE WAS ACTUALLY A PERIOD OF TIME THAT THE BOY COULDN'T REMEMBER.

LEGENDS ARE OFTEN BORN IN SUCH A FASHION.

BURORORORO (VRMMMMM)

WHAT ABOUT THE GAP IN THE BOY'S MEMORIES BEFORE WE FOUND HIM...?

BUT WHAT REALLY HAPPENED?

YOU KNOW... YOU'RE PRETTY LAID BACK.

REALLY?

"HE PRESENTLY ISN'T IN THIS SPACE-TIME."

...WASN'T HE ACTUALLY MISSING FROM THIS SPACE-TIME?

THOSE WORDS...

NOT SURE HOW EXACTLY... BUT IT'D BE EASY ENOUGH FOR NAGATO.

THE BOY'S TIME WAS WARPED BY SOMETHING.

NAGATO, GIVE ME AN HONEST ANSWER.

DID YOU DO "SOMETHING"?

SO WHAT WAS IT FOR?

BUT THIS TIME, I DOUBT THAT HARUHI BELIEVED IN THE EXISTENCE OF A WATER GOD.

WHAT WAS IT FOR? WHAT DID YOU DO?

THE GIRL WAS THE ONE WHO BELIEVED IN A WATER GOD, NOT HARUHI...

I CAN UNDERSTAND YOU ACTING TO MAKE HARUHI HAPPY.

BUT THAT WASN'T THE CASE THIS TIME.

...BEATS ME.

BEATS ME...!?

THAT WAS A SURPRISE.

I DIDN'T EXPECT NAGATO TO REPLY LIKE THAT...

...BEATS...

THERE WAS A FORM OF DISTORTION IN THE AREA CONNECTING THE LAKES.
I MERELY REMOVED THE DISTORTION ...
ANY FURTHER ACTION WOULD BE CONSIDERED SACRILEGE.
....
UNBE-LIEVABLE ...
IS SHE SUGGESTING THAT THERE ACTUALLY IS A WATER GOD?
NO, IT MUST BE TRUE IF SHE SAYS SO...

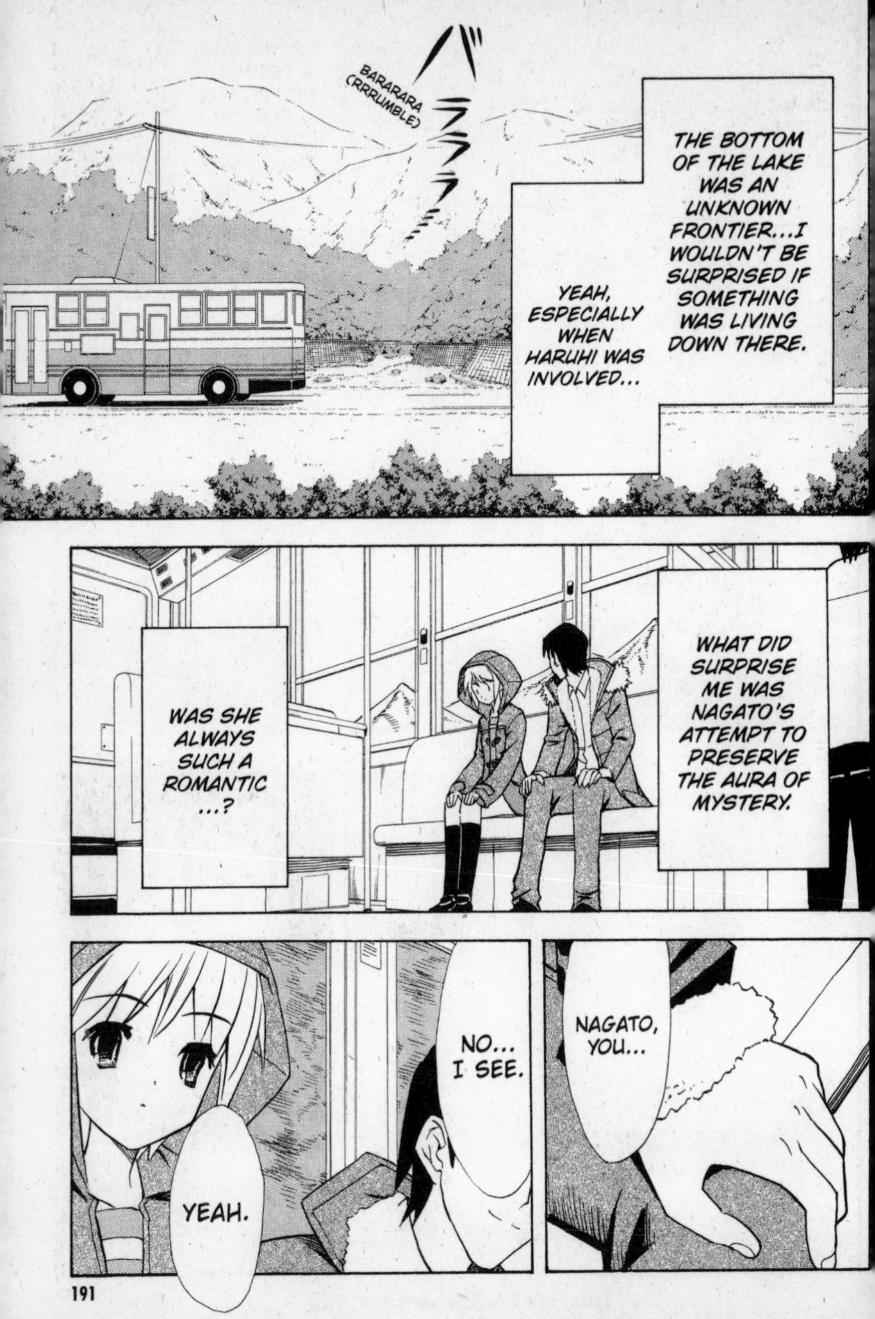
BARARARA (RRRUMBLE)
THE BOTTOM OF THE LAKE WAS AN UNKNOWN FRONTIER...I WOULDN'T BE SURPRISED IF SOMETHING WAS LIVING DOWN THERE.
YEAH, ESPECIALLY WHEN HARUHI WAS INVOLVED...
WHAT DID SURPRISE ME WAS NAGATO'S ATTEMPT TO PRESERVE THE AURA OF MYSTERY.
WAS SHE ALWAYS SUCH A ROMANTIC ...?
NAGATO, YOU...
NO... I SEE.
YEAH.

IT WOULDN'T BE VERY ROMANTIC TO PRESS YOU ANY FURTHER.

SIGN: MITAKE INN

"ONLY THE LAKE KNOWS ALL."
...WE'LL LEAVE IT AT THAT.

Tales From The Thousand Lakes : END

Translation Notes

Page 45

A *zashiki-warashi* is a Japanese spirit that may be found in large, old houses. Having a zashiki-warashi in your home is supposed to bring good fortune, but when the zashiki-warashi leaves, so does your luck. Commonly depicted as a red-faced child, the child-like zashiki-warashi is known for playing tricks, making noises and brief appearances that could almost make you think you had an extra guest in the house, which is exactly how they'd like to be treated.

TO BE CONTINUED

YOU GOTTA BE KIDDING ME...
...I MISSED HARUHI.

THE DISAPPEARANCE OF HARUHI SUZUMIYA

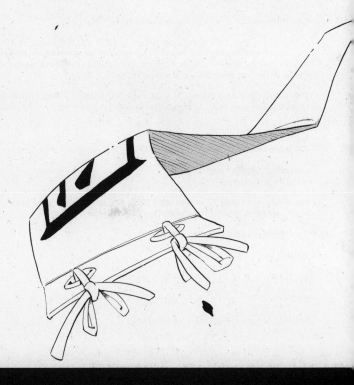

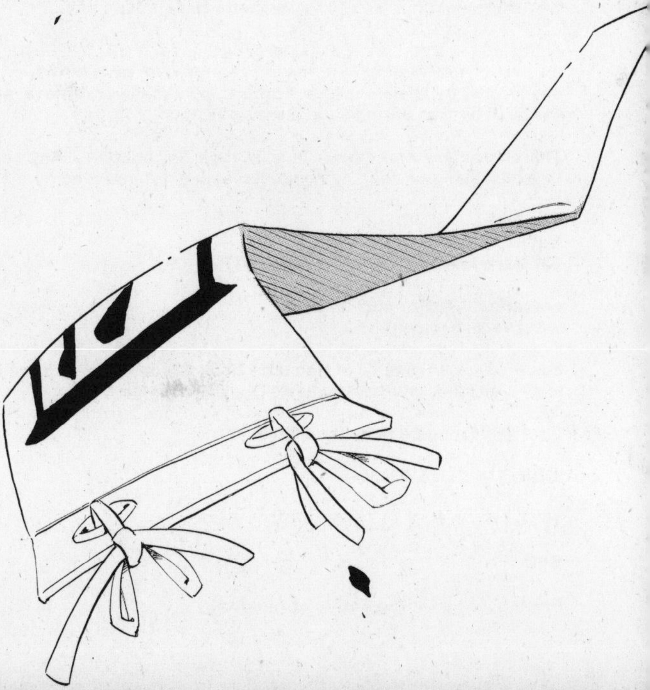

FINALLY ENTERING THE "DISAPPEARANCE" PHASE!

THE MELANCHOLY OF HARUHI SUZUMIYA

6

Original Story: Nagaru Ta
Manga: Gaku Tsugano
Character Design: Noizi It

Translation: Chris Pai for MX Media LLC
Lettering: Alexis Eckerman

Yen Press
Hachette Book Group
237 Park Avenue, New York, NY 10017

www.HachetteBookGroup.com
www.YenPress.com

Yen Press is an imprint of Hachette Book Group, Inc. The Yen Press name and logo are trademarks of Hachette Book Group, Inc.

First Yen Press Edition: June 2010

ISBN: 978-0-316-08952-4

10 9 8 7 6 5 4 3 2 1

BVG

Printed in the United States of America